THE SCOUT GROUP

A Handbook for Group Scout Leaders and Group Administrators

By Dennis Humphries

Edited by Stephen Nixey

Design by Deborah Thompson

Illustrated by Rich

The Scout Association, Baden-Powell House, Queen's Gate, London SW7 5JS

ISBN 0 85165 2921

New Edition

First printing 1996

Printed by Optichrome

CONTENTS

INTRODUCTION

The previous publication, entitled ***The Scout Group***, was rapidly becoming obsolete as the progressive training scheme had changed since the book was printed and, with the rapidly progressing aspect of the inclusion of girls within other Sections of the Movement, other than Venture Scouts, it was necessary to think of updating the information available for Group Scout Leaders and Administrators.

With this in mind it was decided to have a series of articles printed in SCOUTING Magazine which would ultimately be turned into a book format at the conclusion of the series, to provide a replacement for the earlier publication.

This book is the result of those articles by an author who has served The Scout Association in a variety of roles, including those of Group Scout Leader and as a County Administrator, over many years. Thus, the contents are based on personal experiences and are approached from a practical point of view. It is hoped that the book will prove to be of valuable assistance to all those involved in running a Scout Group, as Group Scout Leaders or Administrators, both in the initial reading and as a future reference document.

Of necessity, the guidance given can only be general and much of the advice will have to be adapted to your own circumstances but basic information is in accordance with the rules of the Movement and combined with practical methods of achieving the degree of support that would be expected from a Group Scout Leader or Administrator – appointments that are vital to the successful provision of Scouting for the young people of today.

Scouting is a partnership between the Leaders within the Sections and those – the Group Scout Leader and the Administrators – who provide that vital support to enable the Group to function efficiently and effectively.

This book should be an important resource to aid and support that partnership and together with the many other resources available - SCOUTING Magazine, ***Policy, Organisation and Rules***, Resource Centre material and practical support through training courses within your District or County – Scouting can only develop and flourish for the benefit of all those involved.

It is also appreciated that many who take up the appointments as Group Scout Leaders, Administrators or Managers may not have been involved in Scouting before and, to them, the jargon, the abbreviations and similar that they hear within a Scout Group or District is some what bewildering and off-putting. In this publication, we have endeavoured to overcome that obstacle by referring to all such elements in full.

However, there will be times when abbreviations are used in the normal routine of Scouting – often because of familiarity and ease of use – and simply because the speaker tends to assume that all are familiar with the subject. It is, therefore, recommended that the 'notes' section at the back of this book is used to record these abbreviations and their meanings for future reference.

May you have a very enjoyable time in Scouting in these often unsung and, at times, seemingly unappreciated roles that are none-the-less vital to the Scout Movement.

CHAPTER ONE A HISTORY OF THE SCOUT MOVEMENT

Once upon a time (all the best stories start with those words) a group of people engaged in different roles within the Scout Movement sat down to review the resources needed to assure the successful development of Scouting in their locality over the next ten years.

After much deliberation and thought, they reached the conclusion that the single, most important person in Scouting was the Group Scout Leader. Sadly, However, they also reflected that around 25 per cent of their Scout Groups did not have a Group Scout Leader.

Without a doubt they were not alone in their findings – nor in their resolve that the centre of the Scout Group is the Group Scout Leader and should be recognised by all. To this end, effective support should be provided by a team of Administrators.

Isolating the problem

Having isolated the problem, where are these people to be found? How about one of the other Scout Leaders in the Group taking on the job?

There are many Scouters who do not wish to accept an appointment as Group Scout Leader. They feel, often justifiably, that they are more useful in one or other of the Sections, and much happier to be in contact, week by week, with the young people for whose benefit Scouting exists.

Without the support of the Scout Group as a whole and the Group Scout Leader in particular, they cannot, however, succeed fully. The Group Scout Leader, in turn, cannot do a really good job unless he or she can rely on the enthusiastic and committed support of the various Group Administrators, who have only come to be regarded as full and equal partners in the Scout Group's team of adults in recent years.

Clearly, if the Scout Group is central to Scouting, the Group Scout Leader and Administrators need effective support and guidance in the important roles they are undertaking.

The aim of this book

The aim of this book is to provide the Group Scout Leader and the Administrator with some assistance in discovering what it is they need to be doing.

But where does one start?

A survey carried out a few years ago among the general public revealed a wide divergence of knowledge as to what Scouting is all about.

Whereas, some individuals may have enjoyed Membership of the Scout Movement for a number of years before accepting an appointment, the experience of many may not have extended beyond incurring the wrath of Akela's tongue on their second Pack night.

Many adults only become involved for the first time when their children join the Movement. To be safe then, we will assume you have no knowledge of Scouting at all, and the best place to start is at the very beginning.

History of Scouting

1907: Robert Baden-Powell took 20 boys from various backgrounds to Brownsea Island for a fortnight's experimental camp to test out his ideas.

1908: Scouting for Boys was published in fortnightly parts.

1910: The Guide Association was set up as a separate organisation. The two Associations remain separate today, although their aims and basic principles are almost identical and they do co–operate extensively in many matters, both locally and nationally.

1916: Wolf Cubs were formed. Their programme and organisation was based on **The Jungle Book**, by Rudyard Kipling. Leaders in the Cub Scout Section are still known by 'jungle names' such as Akela and Bagheera.

1918: Rover Scouts were started to cater for young men – mostly former Scouts – who wanted to remain Members of the Scout Movement without necessarily becoming Leaders.

1946: The Senior Scout Section was set up to provide activities for boys aged fifteen to eighteen years who, until then, had been part of the Scout Troop.

1966: The Chief Scout's Advance Party Report was published, following lengthy consultation with Members of the Movement. The Senior Scouts were superseded by Venture Scouts, to cater for the age range of sixteen to twenty years. A number of other changes to the structure, programme and general policy of the Association were made at the same time, such as the adoption of the names 'Cub Scout' and 'Scout' instead of 'Wolf Cub' and 'Boy Scout'.

1982: The Scout Association gave approval for the formation of Beaver Scout Colonies within the Scout Group. Beavers were not initially Members of The Scout Association but merely affiliated to it, but since 1986, as Beaver Scouts they have been full Members alongside their older brothers and sisters.

1990: The Committee of the Council of The Scout Association agreed that the Association should accept the principle of enabling mixed Membership opportunities to be considered as an option by Scout Groups.

Movement cannot stand still

Every time there is a change of policy, the response is to question the need for such action. Is it really necessary? Can't we just stay as we are? Apply the same logic to any consumer product, say a motor car. A model 'T' Ford might be very nice, nostalgically, but it would not be very competitive on the world market.

To be successful, a manufacturer must identify, anticipate and satisfy customers' requirements, positively. Scouting must also constantly undergo re-appraisal to see that it also continues to satisfy the needs of its customers.

Limitations and expectations of society as a whole, and especially young people, are constantly changing. Many of these changes are subtle and the process so gradual that they do not warrant any immediate action but, however minor they may be, these changes – taken over a period – will show a trend. It is within the Scout Group that we will first detect the needs, hopes and even the dissatisfaction of our younger Membership. It is in response to feed-back of these feelings from Scout Groups that The Scout Association reacts.

The very definition of the word 'Movement' denotes action, change and response to the requirements of the Membership. The history of Scouting reflects the way in which the Scout Movement has responded to the needs of the times.

Scouting today

The Scout Movement is one of the greatest and most progressive youth movements in the world today, with over 25 million people world-wide. In the United Kingdom alone, well over half a million people are experiencing the fun, friendship and excitement of Scouting. For over 80 years, the Scout Movement has been providing an enjoyable and attractive scheme of training, aimed at encouraging the physical, intellectual, spiritual and social development of young people. The Scout Association of the United Kingdom, is a multi-cultural, multi-faith organisation, consisting of four sections:

- **Beaver Scouts:** boys and girls aged six to eight years-old.
- **Cub Scouts:** Boys and girls aged eight to ten and-a-half years-old.
- **Scouts:** boys and girls aged ten and-a-half years-old to fifteen and-a-half years-old.
- **Venture Scouts:** Young men and women aged fifteen-and-a-half years old to twenty years-old.

Locally several of these Sections link up to form a Scout Group. In addition to these four Sections are the adult Leaders whose ages range from eighteen to sixty-five years.

Leaders need not have had previous Scouting experience, and training is provided both locally and nationally at Gilwell Park, London. There is also a team of Helpers, Skills Instructors and Administrators who take care of the administrative aspects of running a Scout Group.

Additionally, there is the Scout Fellowship, for individuals aged eighteen years-old upwards – there is no upper age limit – who wish to provide support for local Scouting in over 960 Scout Districts throughout the UK.

As well as having a social function, the Scout Fellowship allows those who cannot give regular commitment, for any reason, to enjoy Membership of The Scout Association.

Scout Fellowship Members support Sections, Groups and Districts in many practical ways at events, with specialised skills within the Sections, at camp sites, with advice and general help as requested and when required.

Training programme

The Scout Association's training programme is progressive and is geared to suit the Membership's wide range of age, experience and ability.

The programme is adaptable, so as to meet the needs of the individual, including those Members with Special Needs.

Scouting activities are about involvement and aims to encourage responsibility, self-reliance, the acquisition of special skills and an appreciation of the world in which we live. The list of activities is endless and may include camping, climbing, parascending, canoeing, abseiling, karting, photography, music, acting, crafts, sailing, caving, skiing and cooking. In fact, there are few activities that are not covered by Scouting at some time.

Involvement with the community is also a very important part of Scouting and Members may take part in activities such as fund raising for charities, conservation projects, litter clearance or give practical help to the elderly and those with special needs.

Aim and Method of The Scout Association

The Scout Association, in the United Kingdom, operates in accordance with a book called ***Policy, Organisation and Rules*** – an essential item in the library of every Scouter and Administrator – and it is at the very beginning, prior to **Rule 1**, that we find a statement of the Aim and the Method of the Association.

The Aim of The Scout Association is to promote the development of young people in achieving their full physical, intellectual, social and spiritual potentials, as individuals, as responsible citizens and as members of their local, national and international communities. The Method of achieving the Aim of the Association is by providing an enjoyable and attractive scheme of progressive training, based on the Scout Promise and Law and guided by adult Leadership.

Everything we do in Scouting is done in furtherance of this Aim and in accordance with this Method.

The importance of teamwork is emphasised throughout the Scout Movement and everyone has his or her part to play.

If we want to see a better world for future generations, how better to achieve it than by helping to mould the lives of those who will be the next generation of adults?

CHAPTER TWO

SCOUT PROMISE AND LAW

If we can accept that the Scout Movement has to change to meet the needs of the times, why do we maintain that most difficult concept, the Promise and Law?

Every Leader must seek out his or her attitude to the Promise and Law and convey this to the young people in their charge in everything that they say or do. Whether they like it or not, society, at large, places all Leaders on a 'pedestal' – maybe not a very big one, but like lawyers and so on, Leaders are expected to live by a code of conduct on a higher plane than the norm.

The Scout Promise

Every Member of the Scout Movement throughout the world, all 25 million of them, have one thing in common – **The Scout Promise**...

On my honour, I promise that I will do my best to do my duty to God and to the Queen, to help other people and to keep the Scout Law.

The words may differ, of course, according to the language, and other minor differences of phrasing between different religions or different systems of government, but the substance is the same throughout the Movement.

In the United Kingdom, Members generally make the promise shown above, but many pay little more than 'lip service' to the Scout Promise as one of the requirements for obtaining full Membership of the Scout Movement, yet it is at the very core of that Movement. Together with the Scout Law, the Promise is the means by which we further the Aim and the Method of The Scout Association.

Cub Scouts make a similar Promise, except that they do not use the words ***On my honour*** and they **keep the Cub Scout Law**. The Beaver Scouts' Promise is made in words more appropriate to their age:

I promise to do my best to be kind and helpful and to love God.

They do not have a Law to keep, but the concepts expressed in the Scout Law are presented to Beaver Scouts by their Leaders through games, story-telling, crafts and other informal activities.

Scouting is available to all faiths and there are variations of the Scout Promise to take account of the different religious obligations of its Members, while upholding the essential spirit of the Promise.

In each Promise, the phrase ***duty to God*** or, in the case of the Beaver Scouts, ***to love God***, is suitable for most faiths (including Christians, Hindus, Muslims and Sikhs). Hindus may use either words, ***my Dharma*** (which refers to Hindu moral law) or ***God***. Orthodox Muslims can use the word ***Allah*** in place of ***God***. Buddhists should use only the words, ***my Dharma*** (which refers to truth).

Similarly, Scouts who are not British subjects and so do not owe allegiance to the Queen will replace the phrase ***duty... to the Queen*** with ***duty... to the country in which I am now living.*** However, the essential message is the same in each case and the making of the Promise is a strict condition of Membership for everyone, no matter what their age or appointment.

When we take the Scout Promise apart and inspect each statement separately we may begin to appreciate its depth of meaning more clearly. The task of putting this concept over to our young people may then become an easier one.

On my honour...

What do we mean by that? We may use the terms ***'swear on the Holy Book'*** and ***'cross my heart'*** when we want other people to really believe what we say. ***On my honour*** means just that, no room for dual standards, saying one thing and doing another. Imagine one of your young Members comes up to you and tells you that they have found a small sum of money. What should they do with it?

... I Promise...

When we make a promise, we usually really mean to keep it, but then, other things crop up which alter the circumstances, and maybe we don't. We have all heard the child say, 'you promised, mum'. The young face will register disappointment at being let down – no amount of excuses will be good enough. After all, mum's promise, perhaps above all others, is to be relied on.

... that I will do my best...

This does not mean that I will do my best at some stage in the future, but that I will do my best all the time. It means being prepared to put oneself out and to make some personal sacrifices to achieve your best. Are we, as Leaders, always achieving our best?

... to do my duty to God...

This does not necessarily mean going to a place of worship every week. Most world religions teach love for one another and any kind act to someone who is in need can loosely be described as ***duty to God***.

Acknowledging that there is a power greater than ourselves, or our comprehension, is acknowledging God.

... and to the Queen...

The Queen is the monarch and the figurehead of the country and, therefore, the representative of the nation and all that that means, for example, law and order. Breaking the law of the land and any number of 'trivial' things we do every day can be anti-social, if not illegal.

... to help other people...

The Scout Movement is part of the world-wide family of Scouts. In many countries around the world it is Scouts who are running the health and education programmes for their communities. The ways in which Scouts in the United Kingdom can help other people starts with the Colony, Pack, Troop or Unit just down the road! Anyone in need is a friend. That person who is never popular, the hyperactive child, hooligan and bully, even those people who seem to have everything or even the dejected vagrant who has nothing.

... and to keep the Scout Law...

What is the Scout Law? Why do we need it?

It is a set of guidelines to help us to live out the Promise in our daily lives.

The Scout Law is in seven parts:

1. A Scout is to be trusted.

2. A Scout is loyal.

3. A Scout is friendly and considerate.

4. A Scout belongs to the world–wide family of Scouts.

5 A Scout has courage in all difficulties.

6. A Scout makes good use of time and is careful of possessions and property.

7. A Scout has self-respect and respect for others.

There is a simpler version of this Law for Cub Scouts (Beaver Scouts do not have a Law), and the concepts involved are presented to them through activities, such as games and story telling.

It should be noted, however, that the Scout Law consists of positive statements, rather than negative ones – for example, that ***a Scout is to be trusted***, and this clearly implies that a person who cannot be trusted is not truly a Scout, no matter how many badges he or she may be wearing.

What are we demanding of our young people when we ask them to keep the Scout Law in today's society? Were the same things socially acceptable when we were youngsters, as are accepted as the norm today? Our views and values may be different from those of our young people, but we must always remember that they are entitled to those views, and respect them.

The Promise and Law are at the very heart of Scouting. It might be possible to run a Scout Group without uniforms or badges, with no headquarters, and with only the barest skeleton of a training programme. It probably would not be a very good Group, but it would still be Scouting of a sort.

A Scout Group without the Promise is a contradiction in terms – if the Promise and Law are not there, it is simply not Scouting but just another youth orientated organisation.

In Baden-Powell's last message, he challenged us, 'Try to leave this world a little better than you found it'. If we all did that, not only those trying to abide by the Scout Promise and Law, but everyone, what a much better world we would be living in.

Religion in Scouting

In making the Scout Promise we accept that there is a being, or a power, greater than ourselves. This being is called by a name – dependant upon the religion – which may be *God*, *Allah* or *my Dharma*, for example.

Making the Scout Promise is an essential condition of Membership and this Promise includes the words, ***duty to God***.

Anyone with no religious belief clearly cannot, honestly, make such a promise and so, cannot become a Scout. But anyone who believes in a God, or other Divine Power can, in all conscience, make the Scout Promise and become a Member of the Scout Movement.

The Scout Promise is not the end, however, for the Aim of The Scout Association speaks of promoting the development of young people in achieving their spiritual potential, and this development is a continuing process.

The religious policy of The Scout Association therefore includes the following statement...

All Members of the Scout Movement are encouraged to:

- **Make every effort to progress in the understanding and observance of the Promise to do their best to do their duty to God.**

- **Belong to some religious body.**

- **Carry into daily practice what they profess.**

Thus, it is part of the role of the Scouts to encourage each Member to follow a religion and to follow whatever obligations this may impose upon them.

An adult makes the Promise and accepts the same religious obligations as a younger Member.

Before recommending the issue of a Leader warrant, the District Commissioner will wish to ensure that the prospective Leader is aware of these obligations. In particular, all Leaders are expected to implement the Association's religious policy by their own personal example.

There are many, especially young people, who are still unsure in their own minds about religious matters, and who have not yet committed themselves wholeheartedly to any religious denomination.

Such a person, who is seriously and conscientiously seeking the truth, and who is prepared to make the Scout Promise, may be appointed to Leadership.

They, like any other Scout Leader or Commissioner, will be responsible for the spiritual development of the young Members in their charge, and it would be almost impossible for them to discharge their responsibility if they had not yet formed any clear spiritual beliefs of their own.

How is this to be done? In most Groups, spiritual development activities include prayers at the beginning or end of Colony, Pack, Troop or Unit meetings, Scout's Own services in camp, or maybe religious parades.

Where Members are of different denominations, this will often take place at various places of worship in the locality. However, it must be clearly understood that attendance at any form of worship must be voluntary. There must also be an understanding that those who do withdraw from prayers, do so in order to carry out their own religious obligations, and not to enjoy extra 'free time'.

Spiritual development should extend beyond mere prayers however, and aspects of spiritual development will occur naturally in any well–balanced programme. Members should be encouraged through ordinary activities to develop an inner discipline and accept high personal standards, to become involved in projects with others, to develop an understanding of the natural world, to help create a tolerant and caring society, to learn about the many forms of worship to be found in today's world, and to find a place for prayer and worship in their own lives.

Hopefully, it will be seen that achieving one's own spiritual potential need not be a separate (or boring) activity – on the contrary, it can be as adventurous and enjoyable as any other part of Scouting.

CHAPTER THREE

THE SCOUT GROUP

It was one of those days at camp when it was so cold and wet, there was little that could be done, other than have a quiz. When the Cub Scouts were asked 'Who is the Chief Scout?', the reply came, 'The Group Scout Leader'. This response would be perfectly logical to the younger Member because it is the Group Scout Leader who is seen as the most important Leader in the Scout Group, the 'head' of the family so to speak.

Before 1927, each Wolf Cub Pack, Scout Troop and Rover Scout Crew registered independently and was treated as a separate entity. It had become apparent, however, that some form of continuity would be advantageous. Indeed, after World War I, Scout Headquarters had actively encouraged the Sections to be aware of each other. In some areas, all three Sections practically formed one unit and the desire was expressed for a suitable name which would embrace all three.

After considering suggestions such as Post, Squadron, or 'Tamasha' – even Baden-Powell's idea, 'Clump' (former designation for a group of halbadiers, spears men and archers), the General Purposes sub-Committee decided on the less romantic, but more practical term, 'Scout Group'. Nearly 70 years on, the Scout Group is still with us!

Why have a Scout Group?

The progressive training scheme must be perceived to be from six years-of-age through to twenty, and not just four separate stages.

The young Member needs to feel confident and happy about going from one Section to another, fostering a 'family' spirit. It is also within the framework of the Scout Group that observance of the Scout Law is nurtured, providing a secure base for the achievement of physical, intellectual, social and spiritual potentials as a responsible citizen.

The current high rate of family breakdown and the issues that arise from this often results in a great number of young people turning to their Leaders for advice and wisdom.

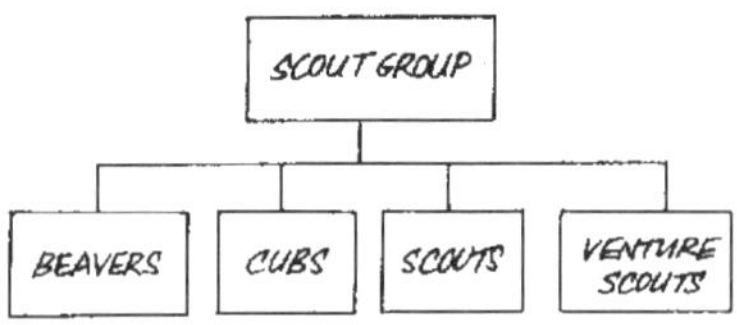

The Scout Group is a structural mechanism that works.

What is a Scout Group?

Today, the complete Scout Group contains a Beaver Scout Colony, (for young people aged six to eight years), a Cub Scout Pack (for young people aged eight to ten-and-a-half years, with the upper age limit being eleven years, depending on circumstances), a Scout Troop (for young people aged ten-and-a-half to fifteen-and-a-half years, with a similar flexible transfer as for the Cub Scouts), and a Venture Scout Unit (for young men and women aged fifteen-and-a-half to twenty years of age). Some Scout Groups may be larger than this, with more than one Colony, Pack or Troop, whilst others may be smaller, and not have a full complement of Sections.

Each Group, however, should be supported by a Group Council of Administrators, parents and friends.

A Scout Group working properly is the fundamental way of Scouting in this country.

A number of Scout Groups in a given geographical area constitutes a District.

In rural areas, this number may be as low as five or six Groups. In towns, it may be as many as 15 or more.

The organisation and functions of the District will be described fully later but, essentially, the District Team (consisting of a District Commissioner and several other experienced Leaders) exists to support the work of the Scout Groups.

In turn, a number of Districts make up a County (called an Area in Scotland and Wales). This usually coincides with a local government administrative county, but may be a sub division – made up from a number of urban authorities.

The County structure and County Team is very similar to that of the District and has similar functions.

A Scout Group, as has been stated, consists of one or more Sections and, in normal circumstances, the aim should be to form a complete Group with all the separate Sections present.

It must be recognised, however, that this is not always possible – some village Groups may consist of a Beaver Scout Colony or a Cub Scout Pack only, for example, with Scouts transferring to another larger Group in a nearby village or town.

Some Groups may be sponsored by a boarding school, and are thus limited to the age range of the pupils. many Scout Groups do not have a Venture Scout Unit, but instead encourage their older Scouts to join the local Venture Scout Unit, which may be able to provide a wider selection of activities.

There will always be special cases of this sort, but as a general guideline, a Scout Group should aim to cater for the whole age range.

There is no restriction on the overall size of a Scout Group, but practical consideration must be taken into account. A Cub Scout Pack and a Scout Troop is unlikely to function efficiently with fewer than 12 Members, and a Beaver Scout Colony and Venture Scout Unit will need at least eight Members if it is to carry out a worthwhile programme. On the other hand, the maximum size of a Colony is 24 Beaver Scouts, and a Pack 36 Cub Scouts – a Scout Group may, however, have two or even three Cub Scout Packs or Beaver Scout Colonies, as long as adequate facilities and Leadership is available. A Scout Group may, thus, vary in size from less than thirty, to well over a hundred Members.

Membership of a Scout Group may be of either single or mixed sex Sections, as decided by the Group Scouters' Meeting and the Group Executive Committee, Patrol Leaders' Council and the Unit Executive.

When making this decision, the Scout Group must discuss it with the existing Membership. It is a decision taken by the whole Scout Group and not the individual Sections. Progress through the Sections must be available to all Members and once it has been agreed to have mixed membership, the decision is not reversible.

Girls in Scouting/ Co-education

It may be useful to mention at this stage one or two other points relating to mixed membership.

Female or mixed Leadership teams are required when the Membership of Colonies, Packs and Troop are of a mixed Membership. In the event of there being only one female Leader, who then leaves for some reason, the District Commissioner (after consultation with the Group Scout Leader) must be satisfied with arrangements which are being made to involve a female Leader during the interim period.

Any camp or holiday for a mixed Pack or Troop must have an adult female amongst the Leadership team. Support to fulfil these requirements can come from Helpers, parents, Members of the Scout Fellowship or other suitable adults (on completion of **WE** procedure) as well as Warranted Leaders.

In a mixed Troop, it is also highly desirable that a female Leader or other female adult is present at all other times. For mixed Patrol camps or expeditions, a female adult should be available in the location or vicinity.

Registration

When a Scout Group is first registered at Headquarters, it is issued with a registration card giving the title of the Scout Group, its date of registration, whether or not it is a Sponsored Group (see next chapter) and a registration number.

At one time, this number was of little use other than intrinsic value to determine seniority – nowadays, this becomes the identification number for the Scout Group on the computer records. The Group will change as the years go by – some Leaders will inevitably leave and others will be appointed, new Sections may be added or even closed, the Group may even change its meeting place, if so desired.

For obvious reasons, it would be sensible to let potential visitors know of any such changes, but the details on the registration card cannot be changed without a formal application being made by the District to Headquarters.

The registration number, therefore, comes into particular importance with the Annual Census. Some Scout Groups also like to remember the registration date and even hold a party, or other special event, on the anniversary of this date.

As to the choice of the title for a new Scout Group, most Districts have a local policy on this matter and the Group is likely to be asked to conform by adopting a specific style of name. Some titles may involve a number and a name, such as the 29th Bomere Heath, or it may be that the District identify with names only, for example, Shuttleworth (All Saints) Scout Group, where the name of the Sponsoring Authority appears in the title.

Sponsored Groups

In the last chapter we mentioned Sponsored Scout Groups – there are two types of Scout Group, often referred to as Sponsored, or Open.

The Open group, which is by far the more common, stands independent of any outside organisation and has a policy of unrestricted recruitment, subject only to the rules of The Scout Association.

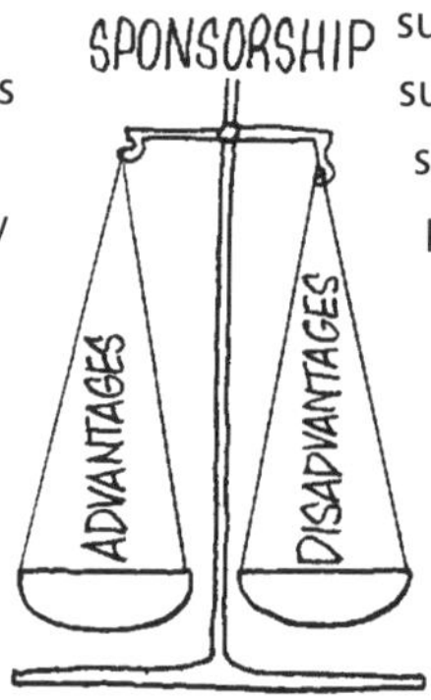

Secondly, there is what is known as the Sponsored Group, sponsored by an organisation such as religious body, a school or an industrial concern. Most Sponsored Scout Groups have an unrestricted recruitment policy no different from that of an Open Group, but a few operate a policy of restricted recruitment, laid down by the Sponsoring Authority as agreed with the District. A District Commissioner can request that Membership of a Sponsored Group be restricted.

The question of sponsorship is one that calls for serious consideration, because it can bring with it both advantages and disadvantages for the Scout Group. Depending upon the terms of the Sponsorship Agreement, the Sponsoring Authority may be prepared to provide accommodation and other facilities for the use of the Scout Group, to offer financial assistance, to assist in finding suitable Leaders, and/or to support in various ways, the spiritual aspects of the training programme.

On the other hand, the Sponsoring Authority has a right to be consulted on various matters concerning the Membership or status of the Scout Group, and may wish to restrict the recruitment of Members and/or Leaders (for example, to active members of a particular religious body).

All these matters must be agreed between the Sponsoring Authority and the District Chairman (on behalf of the District Executive Committee) when the Sponsored Scout Group is first registered as such, and embodied in a formal written agreement, setting out responsibilities of the Sponsoring Authority in accordance with ***Policy, Organisation and Rules***.

This agreement must then be reviewed at least every five years, or more often if there is a change of Sponsoring Authority (for example, a new religious leader) or Group Scout Leader. It may also be reviewed at any time upon the request of either party. One thing is clear however, and that is, that the training of Members, in all matters, is the responsibility of the Group Scout Leader and the team of Scouters. It is not for the Head Teacher or the religious leader to say, for example, when a camp may be held or who can attend – that is a training matter for Scouters alone.

At the same time, it must be recognised that conflicts may arise between (say) weekend activities and attendance at a place of worship or school football matches, and the wise Group Scout Leader will try to ensure that such clashes, inevitable as they may be, are resolved with a minimum of ill feeling on either side. Particular mention must be made of the Scout Group sponsored by a school, whether a boarding school or otherwise.

If the Leaders are Members of the school staff (as is often the case), they may find it difficult (as may the youngsters) to switch at four o'clock from a teacher/pupil to a Scouter/Scout relationship, which is something quite different. For this reason, it is essential that Membership of school-sponsored Scout Groups should be entirely voluntary, and highly desirable that some or all of the Scouters should be people who are not teachers of that particular school.

The decision as to whether or not a Scout Group will be sponsored must be made with care – once made, it can only be changed by a formal change in the Group's registration, requiring the agreement of the Sponsoring Authority. However, many newly formed Scout Groups in particular have found that sponsorship has brought with it facilities and resources that they would have been hard pressed to obtain on their own.

Amalgamation and closure

Sadly, the time may come when a particular Scout Group is no longer able to function properly. This can be caused by circumstances beyond anyone's control, for example, where there has been a shift in a community's population due to a major employer moving their centre of operations to another part of the country.

For whatever reason the Group is now no longer viable, and in spite of the most determined of efforts by the Group Council and the District Team to find alternative arrangements, it may be considered necessary to close the Group or to amalgamate with a neighbouring Scout Group – maybe a more successful one. Two Cub Scout Packs, each with one Leader and nine young Members may have little chance of success, after all, but one Pack with two Leaders and 18 Members can achieve all sorts of things.

A short term possibility, if the District Commissioner considers that a Group's problems are of a temporary nature, is that it may be allowed to become dormant. In this case, the Group ceases to hold meetings, and its assets and property are temporarily frozen, to be released if and when the Group resumes operations. A Scout Group cannot remain dormant for more than a year, however, if there is still no rescue after that time it will have to be closed.

An amalgamation is not a take over – it normally means that both of the former Groups are officially closed and a new one opened. However, because of the legal implications and statutory regulations which must be observed, amalgamation is a complex business and should not be considered lightly. If it is required to change the registration of a Scout Group, for example, by proposing to amalgamate with another Group, Form **C2** must be submitted to Headquarters by the District Secretary.

But that is not all. The amalgamation of a Sponsored Scout Group with another Group, may take place only with the full consent of the Sponsoring Authority, if a Sponsored Scout Group meets the minimum standards for Scout Groups. If the Sponsoring Authority does not desire amalgamation with another Group, these wishes must be respected. In the event of a disagreement, the matter must be referred to the District Commissioner and both the Sponsoring Authority and the Group Scout Leader must be given reasonable opportunity to state their cases.

Further, the Administrators of a Scout Group must concern themselves with all the legal requirements regarding the ownership of all property and equipment and to the hiring of premises. This includes the appointment of Trustees and adopting correct procedures for the discharging of responsibilities. Therefore, before doing anything at all it is strongly recommended that a careful study is made of the appropriate passages in ***Policy, Organisation and Rules***.

Likewise the dismissal of a Member of a Scout Group, be they a Beaver Scout, Cub Scout, Scout or Venture Scout, is based on the judgement of the Group Scout Leader. In a Sponsored Group, the Sponsoring Authority must be consulted before any such dismissal takes place. If a Member is dismissed they have the right to appeal against this decision, as laid down in ***Policy, Organisation and Rules.***

CHAPTER FIVE THE SECTIONS – BEAVER SCOUTS AND CUB SCOUTS

One of the pleasures of being a grandparent is that you can spoil your grandchildren rotten, then hand them back to their parents when they become fractious.

It can be like that being a Group Scout Leader. There may be occasions, when some, or all of the Leaders in a Section are away on holiday, or ill, or on training courses, and then it may well be the Group Scout Leader who steps into the breach to run (or help to run) the weekly meeting.

In the case of the grandparent, one will have experience as a parent to fall back on, whereas the Group Scout Leader may not be lucky enough to have had first-hand practice in one of the Sections. In the case of the Scout Troop or the Venture Scout Unit, of course, the Group Scout Leader's role would be little more than that of an onlooker, with the programme being run largely by the Members themselves. Pack or Colony meetings would call for rather more active participation on the Group Scout Leader's part.

It is important, for several reasons, that the Group Scout Leader should understand how each of the Sections functions, even though he or she is not directly responsible for any one of them. Whilst the Group Scout Leader's role is to advise and encourage the Section Leaders and their Assistants, such advice based on total ignorance is rarely welcome and usually worthless. Also, one hopes that the Group Scout Leader will be a reasonably frequent visitor to the various Section meetings, and it is well to know a little about what is going on so that appropriate words of congratulation and encouragement can be offered.

The Beaver Scout Colony

The Beaver Scout Section is the newest Section of the Scout Movement and caters for youngsters aged six to eight years-old.

Each Beaver Colony can normally take up to a maximum of 24 youngsters, however, to meet local circumstances this number may be increased, and they are divided into working units called 'Lodges'. Colonies can exist independently and feed to any suitable Scout Group or, preferably, should be part of a Scout Group where progression through the sections is possible.

There is a relatively informal programme of activities in a Beaver Scout meeting – games, craftwork, outings and similar, based on a variety of methods, underpinned by some key principles, administered under the guidance of an adult Beaver Scout Leader and Assistant Beaver Scout Leaders.

Uniform consists of a grey Beaver Scout sweatshirt with embroidered Beaver Scout motif, a turquoise or Group scarf, a maroon woggle, Group name tape, County and District badges, the World Membership Badge and, after an appropriate time the two Beaver Scout programme badges.

The Beaver Scout Colony should have a fairly substantial staff – looking after two dozen energetic six and seven year-olds is by no means an easy job!

There should be at least two adults for each Colony, one of whom will be a Warranted Beaver Scout Leader, with overall responsibility for the management of the Colony. It is strongly recommended that another should be an Assistant Beaver Scout Leader, also holding a Warrant, and be capable of taking over responsibility if the Beaver Scout Leader should be absent for any reason.

Other adults may also be appointed, as Skills Instructors, by the District Commissioner, or as Helpers, by the Section Leader with the approval of the Group Scout Leader, District Commissioner and Appointments sub-Committee.

Helpers in the Group may be responsible for particular activities but do not have a management role. A Beaver Scout Colony with mixed Membership should have mixed Leadership.

To find a level of formality sufficiently divorced from school, but without over familiarity, special Colony names are often used. These are commonly based on a theme such as animals (otter, squirrel, owl), colours (Brown Beaver, Grey Beaver) and so on.

Lodges or teams

For some activities, it is easier to divide the Colony into smaller groups – such groups or teams are called 'Lodges' and are identified by names based on a common theme, for example, trees (oak, ash, beech), seasons (spring, summer, autumn, winter), rivers (Avon, Dee,

Ouse) or anything else with which the Colony feels comfortable. The key to all this is flexibility.

Colony meetings

Most Beaver Scout Colonies meet once a week, some directly after school or in the early part of the evening, or even on Saturday mornings, as governed by local circumstances.

Beaver Scout training involves a two year experience for the Beaver Scout where all activities are of equal importance. The Colony's Leaders have to ensure the weekly meetings consist of a variety of activities planned with the Aim of The Scout Association foremost in their minds.

This sometimes makes the planning of programmes more difficult, but Beaver Scout Leaders have proved themselves to be very resourceful in planning varied programmes on themes which retain the interest of their Members.

Meetings will probably begin with a simple opening ceremony, though not a Flag Break. After this, there will be games and activities to develop the Beaver Scouts' learning skills and helping them to find out about themselves, others, nature, the world of people and God.

The new Beaver Scout will receive the Beaver Scout Membership Badge in the form of the World Membership Badge upon completion of the basic requirements.

There are also two Beaver Scout badges which are issued by the Beaver Scout Leader after consecutive periods of six to eight months, during which the Beaver Scout must take part in an active and balanced Colony programme. In addition to these, a Beaver Scout may also gain a badge on completion of the Beaver Scout Challenge, an optional award, which should be completed during the Beaver Scout's last few months in the Colony.

Many Colonies make a point of celebrating the Beaver Scouts' birthdays as they come around, and every so often there will be another reason for celebration as one of the Members is given a Beaver Scout badge.

The Cub Scout Pack

The Cub Scout Section caters for youngsters aged eight to ten and-a-half years, with the upper age limit being flexible up to eleven years. There is a full and progressive programme of activities with badges and awards to be gained.

Cub Scout Packs can have up to a maximum of six Sixes, that is 36 Cub

Scouts which are divided into working units called 'Sixes' which, as the name suggests, usually consists of six Members under the control of a Sixer.

The Cub Scout Pack is run by the Cub Scout Leader (Akela) and a number of Assistant Cub Scout Leaders who adopt 'jungle names' from Rudyard Kipling's **The Jungle Book** stories on which Cub Scouting was originally based.

Uniform consists of a green sweatshirt and appropriate trousers as agreed by the Group Scout Leader, the Group scarf held by a woggle in the colour of the Six to which the Cub Scout belongs, Group name tape, County and District badges, the World Membership Badge, Activity Badges and progressive Awards.

The Leader of the Cub Scout Pack is the Cub Scout Leader – more usually known as 'Akela'. He or she should have at least one Assistant Cub Scout Leader holding a Leader Warrant and other assistants such as Skills Instructors or Helpers. A Cub Scout Pack with mixed Membership should have mixed Leadership. Each of these helpers will probably have a Pack name taken from **The Jungle Book** – the most common are 'Baloo', 'Bagheera', 'Kaa' and 'Kim' (albeit this comes in a different book altogether).

There is little excitement over the choice of name for the Sixes, into which a Pack is divided. Each Six is named and identified by a coloured woggle, and is led by a Cub Scout called a Sixer. The Sixer will wear a badge on the right arm bearing two gold bars, their assistant (the Second) has just one gold bar.

Cub Scouts are still at an age where the programme must be largely adult–directed but, from time to time, the Sixers – and sometimes the Seconds – meet with Leaders in the Sixers' Meeting. This has no executive power, unlike the Patrol Leaders' Council in the Scout Troop, but exists as an informal meeting to discuss matters that may affect the Pack.

The training programme

After Investiture, the Cub Scout will start work on the Cub Scout Progressive Training Scheme which is based on three main Awards – the Cub Scout Award, the Adventure Award and the Adventure Crest Award. Other awards available are – the Cub Scout Challenge Award, Scout Family Badges and Activity Badges.

The Cub Scout Challenge Award, as the name suggests, provides a challenge for the older Cub Scout and a lower age limit of nine and-a-half years must be attained before the Cub Scout can start on any of the activities to gain this special award. The four Scout Family Badges are separate badges and are an integral part of the training scheme. They provide a wider knowledge of The Scout Association and enhance the theme of the 'family of Scouts'.

While taking part in activities for progress in the main awards, a Cub Scout may also gain Activity Badges. These badges encourage the individual to develop further the skills in one of the main award badges.

The Pack meeting

Cub Scout training takes place largely through games, and the casual observer may be forgiven for thinking that only a few minutes of a Pack meeting is spent in learning anything. The good Cub Scout Leader, however, will have ensured that the games were played with a purpose, because the Cub Scouts will learn more willingly when they are enjoying themselves.

A typical Pack night programme will include fun, activity and just a little work. Different Packs will have different approaches, but there is usually a game of some sort as the Cub Scouts arrive. The formal start of most Pack meetings will be the Grand Howl (a ceremony which may startle those hearing it for the first time!) followed by the breaking of the Union flag. Many Cub Scout Packs have an inspection, too, at this time. Again, this may be arranged in the format of a game.

The rest of the meeting is spent on games – some active, to work off surplus energy, others quieter, to exercise the mind rather than the body and practical activities of various kinds with, perhaps, very little formal instruction. Some of the activities may be undertaken by the whole Pack together, but more often the Cub Scouts will be working in small groups.

Towards the end of the meeting, the Pack may come together again for a yarn told by one of the Leaders or by a visitor – this is a favourite role for the Group Scout Leader – before the final flag down, prayers and dismissal.

Often, however, the Pack meeting may take an entirely different form, with all the games and other activities having a special theme. Then there will be the occasional weekend activities too, a day trip to a place of interest or to a camp site for a day's Scouting out of doors – or maybe, even a Pack holiday or camp.

CHAPTER SIX THE SECTIONS – SCOUTS AND VENTURE SCOUTS

Its now time for us to turn to the Scout Troop and the Venture Scout Unit to take a closer look at what goes on in these two Sections of the Movement.

The Scout Troop

The Scout Section caters for young people from the age of ten and-a-half years to fifteen and-a-half years. The Scout Troop comprises of Patrols of up to eight Members in number, including a Patrol Leader and a Assistant Patrol Leader.

The Troop is run by the Patrol Leaders Council with the support of the Leaders, who share the running of the programme, look after Troop standards and the general running of the Troop.

Uniform consists of green shirt or sweatshirt, Group scarf, woggle and trousers with the colour and style agreed within the Troop by the Patrol Leaders' Council and after consultation with the Troop Membership, bearing in mind the image of The Scout Association.

The programme covers a spectrum of activities encompassing basic Scout craft, community work, camping,

hi-tech, including computers and amateur radio, international and cultural exchanges, hiking expeditions, climbing, abseiling and both air and water activities.

There are also speciality branches – Sea Scouts and Air Scouts – where predominance is given to special interests in water or air activities in conjunction with the basic Scout programme requirements.

At the very heart of the Troop organisation lies the Patrol system. This is the feature of Scout training which, together with the Promise and Law, makes the Scout and Guide Movements unique among other youth organisations.

In historical terms, there were Patrols of Scouts before there were Troops, so there can be no such thing as a Scout Troop in which the Patrol system does not operate. Without the Patrol system it is simply not Scouting!

The Scout Troop, of course, has its adult Leaders like other Sections. There may also be Skills Instructors and Helpers, but most important are the Patrol Leaders, for it is they who are primarily responsible for the Troop's programme and administration. This responsibility is exercised through the Patrol Leaders' Council (Patrol Leader and Senior Patrol Leader – if appointed – with Scouters present only as advisers) which meets fairly regularly to plan programmes, to award the various training awards as appropriate and, generally make day to day decisions necessary for the smooth running of the Scout Troop.

The Scout Progressive Award Training Scheme

This comprises of four progressive training awards – the Scout Award, the Pathfinder Award, the Explorer Award and the Chief Scout's Award. The first two are designed for the younger Scout, whilst the latter two are for the older Scout. Three other awards are available – the Patrol Activity Award, the Leadership Award and the Chief Scout's Challenge.

Much of the Scout Troop's work is directed in one way or another towards the main Scout camp or expedition, which is generally regarded as the high point of the year. There are other aspects to the programme too – games, service projects, cultural activities and so on.

Venture Scout Unit

The Venture Scout Unit caters for young people aged fifteen and-a-half to twenty years of age and is, essentially, a self–programming unit, under the Leadership of two Venture Scout Leaders (with at least one holding a Warrant). With support and guidance from the Leaders, the running of the Unit is achieved through the Unit Executive Committee, comprising of Members of the Unit, taking on the roles of Chairman, Secretary, Treasurer and other roles as decided by the Unit Membership.

Uniform consists of beige shirt, a dark brown tie or Group scarf, woggle, and mushroom trousers. A brown leather belt may be worn bearing the Scout Badge. A Venture Scout may also wear the Chief Scout's Challenge belt buckle, if gained, up until the Venture Scout Award or Explorer Belt is obtained.

The varied programme covers the full spectrum of activities as listed for the Scout Section, although greater emphasis is placed on looking at social, cultural and issues of health.

After first earning the Venture Scout Award, the ultimate goal of any Venture Scout lies in gaining the Queen's Scout Award, which is the pinnacle of achievement within the Section and represents much hard and dedicated work within the community, the Movement and at a personal level.

As well as working within their own communities, Venture Scouts have mounted a number of major expeditions to help the less privileged of the developing world in places such as Kenya, Sri Lanka, Ghana and Nepal, with the individual Members having to finance their own specialist skills, expedition training, travel and subsistence expenses.

In the next chapter, we turn to the role of Administrators and delve into the world of Group Executive committees to take a look at some of the jobs and important tasks that this group of people undertake.

CHAPTER SEVEN

ROLES IN THE SCOUT GROUP

The very life blood of Scouting is the men and women who are prepared to give up some of their spare time to provide Scouting in Beaver Scout Colonies, Cub Scout Packs, Scout Troops and Venture Scout Units. But it goes beyond this – 'For Scouting to succeed there is a very real need for good financial support, reasonably efficient administration and arrangements made to ensure that property, money, facilities and equipment are all looked after properly', writes Ted Hayden in **Supporting Scouting**.

Uniformed Sections

Each Section should have a Warranted Leader who will have overall responsibility for the management of that Section. There should also be an Assistant Leader who is able to take over responsibility if the Section Leader should be absent for any reason. Some other adults may also be required, subject to the need and availability. There may be specialist Skills Instructors, appointed by the District Commissioner, or Helpers in the Group, appointed by the Group Scout Leader and responsible for particular activities, but without a managerial role. The major contribution from these persons is the provision of Scouting for young people. If, in addition to this, these adults are required to provide administration and financial support for the Scout Group they will be justified in considering themselves to be overloaded. Thus, the Scout Movement provides a system of Administrators to provide the necessary resources for the provision of quality Scouting to our young people.

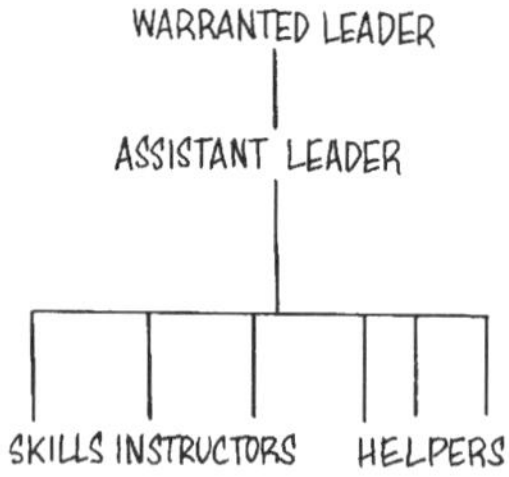

Group Scout Leader

Heading up this company is the Group Scout Leader, who is the Leader of the whole Group. It is the Group Scout Leader's responsibility to knit together a team of adults comprising of Scouters, Helpers and Administrators who will ensure that any young person joining the Scout Group will get the best possible Scouting that can be offered.

Where no Group Scout Leader exists the District Commissioner will appoint a Group Scout Leader (Acting).

Ideally, the Group Scout Leader should not be expected to administrate, nor be the Leader of a Training Section.

The Group Scout Leader is the leader of a team of adults and is very much a manager who can encourage everybody to get on with their own jobs and not try to do the job for them!

All to often, within the Scout Group, there is confusion over who should be doing what, thus a brief description of the roles may prove useful.

Group Chairman

The Group Chairman leads the administrative and support team and, is responsible for the provision of good administration and support for the whole Group. The Group Chairman and the Group Scout Leader should be a partnership.

Group Treasurer

Every Group needs a good book-keeper to ensure the accounts are kept properly, but again, the Treasurer's job goes beyond that.

The Group Treasurer is the financial adviser to the Group and that advice should be available, not only to the Group Executive Committee, but to the Group Scouter's meeting – and even to the Venture Scout Unit Executive and the Patrol Leaders' Council. Budgets, too, come within the responsibility of the Group Treasurer.

As with any other position, Administrators need to be briefed on taking up their posts. In too many cases, a person is left to find out what the responsibilities of the job are. A recent 'straw poll' amongst District Commissioners made it very clear that far too many Group Administrators are not provided with an adequate briefing before appointment. Just under 40 per cent of District Commissioners admitted that such a briefing was minimal or non–existent. Another 40 per cent described their briefing as 'better than minimal, but still not good'. Only 20 per cent claimed that briefing in their District was good.

Group Secretary

The Group Secretary is responsible for the minutes of the Group Council, including the Annual General Meeting, and the meetings of the Group Executive Committee. This is

an important responsibility but, in too many cases, it is all the Group Secretary is required to do. The job however, entails much more than this.

In addition to minutes, the Group Secretary is very much responsible for organising those same meetings. The Group Secretary is the 'right-hand' person to the Group Chairman, offering advice and knowledge of administrative matters in the Scout Movement, so, everybody in the Group will look to the Group Secretary for help and advice in these areas. Just to make sure that the Group Secretary has enough to do, one can add the completion of the Annual Census return to the list of responsibilities.

Annual Registration and Census Return

Groups only exist so long as they are registered as recognised units by The Scout Association. This is done annually and the paperwork is sent to the Group Secretary for completion. In many Groups, the Group Scout Leader sees it as his or her responsibility, when it can easily be completed by the Group Secretary and thus allow the Group Scout Leader to get on with the business of offering real leadership to the Group.

It need not be too difficult a chore. If, for example, the Group Scout Leader reminds the Scouters at the beginning of the month, that the Group Secretary will be on to them for details of their Section, then in any reasonably organised Section this should take about five minutes. In case of any questions about which Section the individual belongs to because he/she is waiting to move up, the answer is that any Beaver Scout awaiting formal Investiture as a Cub Scout should be included as a Cub Scout – and the formula applies right through the Group family.

The Group Scout Leader will need to supply the number of Leaders, leaving out any Venture Scouts who may also double-up as Helpers or Skills Instructors, but include any Helpers or Skills Instructors who are neither Venture Scouts nor Ranger Guides. Leaders who have not yet received their Warrants should also be included.

Some Districts hold a 'Collection Evening' wherein all the Groups come together on the same evening to return their figures to the District Secretary. It gives everyone the opportunity to get together, iron out any difficulties and discuss the figures. This also encourages a sense of team-spirit because any Group late in with figures can hold up the District Returns and, in turn, the County. After this, it is over to the Group Treasurer to sort out the payment of the Membership Subscriptions. Membership subscriptions are not payable for Administrators, therefore, if an Administrator is a Member of the Scout Fellowship, the money should be paid there.

Annual General Meeting

This is the most important thing that the Group Secretary does – again, not the Group Scout Leader's job. Ideally this task would be divided up into three parts. First, the relatively formal business meeting, under the Chairmanship of the Group Chairman. Second, an opportunity, probably during a period for refreshments, for those attending to meet together. In some parts of the country this is one of the few chances to come together because of the distances involved. Finally, a presentation of Scouting activities. This is the responsibility of the Group Scout Leader.

At the Annual General Meeting, the Group Chairman reports what the Executive has done in the past year. If the Group Scout Leader wishes to make any report, it should be concerned with putting forth what the Sections will do in the coming year, thus setting the challenge for the new Executive to meet those needs. It is not the occasion for the Group Scout Leader to give a detailed report on the year and activities. Some other event – for example, a parents' evening – should be convened for this.

Budgets

Quite clearly, if the Executive is going to be expected to support the Training Sections in their activities, then it will be necessary to prepare a budget.

Everyone who incurs expenditure in the course of their duties, including administration and postage, should be asked to provide an accurate assessment of what they are likely to spend in the financial year. The best way to do this is to start from scratch each year and think each item through, taking into account any special events and local or national anniversaries. Alternatively, one can take last year's budget and add a percentage for inflation, quicker, but likely to be less accurate.

Sectional budgets should be agreed with the Group Scout Leader individually before being presented as a whole by the Group Secretary to the Group Executive.

Group Executive Committee

What is the Group Executive? The Group Executive is a Committee which supports the Group Scout Leader and in addition to the raising and administration of Group funds, is responsible for the maintenance of Group property, as well as assisting in other ways.

Every Scout Group should have an effective Executive Committee otherwise the responsibilities fall heavily upon the shoulders of the uniformed Leaders. They should be getting on with the important task of running the Training Sections, not attending meetings.

The Group Scouters' meeting is the vehicle for the Group's Leaders to meet. If necessary, for the purpose of reporting to the Executive, the Group Secretary could possibly attend these meetings.

Alternatively, the minutes of the Group Scouters' meeting could be passed to the Executive.

Too many Group Executives are top heavy with Scouters, whereas they should be looking for the accountants, solicitors, computer specialists and other experts in the field of management and administration amongst the parents of the Group.

CHAPTER EIGHT

MEETINGS

Just imagine going to the Royal Albert Hall to see a Promenade Concert and finding one man on the stage with several instruments strapped to his body, doing his best to play the 1812 Overture! Such a one-man band would appear comical in such a situation and, although doing his best, would not appear terribly effective. All too often, this absurdity becomes a reality in Scouting!

There are still some Scout Groups in which, hopefully not as bad as this, Warranted Leaders are expected to try to do far too many things, such as fund raising, when they should be getting on with their job of training young people and leaving such activities to the Group Council.

Group Council

The Group Council is the body from which most of the Scout Group's support will come. It is a family unit providing adult support, with the Group Scout Leader, the head of that family. All adult Members of the Group (as well as Patrol Leaders and Venture Scouts) are members of the Group Council, as are parents of Beaver Scouts, Cub Scouts, Scouts and Venture Scouts. In the case of the sponsored Group, the Sponsoring Authority will be represented on the Group Council as will other members of the community who wish to identify themselves with the Scout Group and offer their support. Other supporters may be appointed as members by the Group Scout Leader, the Group Executive Committee, or the Group Council itself. The potential of such a body may be quite considerable.

Annual General Meeting

Although there may be other meetings of the Group Council, the one meeting of the year which must take place is the Annual General Meeting. Ideally, this should take place around April to May, as soon as possible after the end of the financial year on March 31, and the date should be fixed and announced to everybody well in advance.

The Annual General Meeting allows the Group Council to receive the Group Executive Committee's Annual Report and Financial Statement for the year just ended, and to elect certain officers and members of the Committee for the coming year.

The Agenda should be in the hands of all the members of the Group Council at least two weeks before the meeting. Items which should be on the Agenda include:

- Minutes of the previous Annual General Meeting.
- Approval of the Annual Report and Accounts.
- Approval of the Group Scout Leader's nomination of Group Chairman.
- Approval of the Group Scout Leader's nomination of members of the Group Executive Committee.
- Election of Group Secretary.
- Election of Group Treasurer.
- Election of members of the Group Council to the Executive Committee.
- Appointment of auditors.

Those people who are in the position of attending several Annual General Meetings, such as the District Commissioner, will be all too familiar with some of the pitfalls of the Annual General Meeting.

Firstly, the Group Scout Leader nominates the Group Chairman. Therefore, the Group Council does not elect the Chairman but approves (or otherwise) the Group Scout Leader's nomination. The Group Secretary and Group Treasurer are elected by the Group Council. To retain maximum attention, the business part of the Annual General Meeting should be limited to a maximum of 45 minutes. It is polite to invite the District Commissioner to say a few words.

The Annual General Meeting may be a good opportunity to make a presentation of Scouting activities available. The presentation may be managed by the Group Scout Leader.

If the Beaver Scouts, Cub Scouts, Scouts or Venture Scouts are going to participate in such a presentation of Scouting in the Group, then care will need to be taken over the timing of the event and something laid on to amuse them while the formal part of the Annual General Meeting is progressing.

Clearly, the Annual General Meeting needs to move smoothly and this is not difficult to achieve providing some thought has been given to it beforehand.

Many Scout Groups hold a planning meeting prior to the event involving say, the Group Scout Leader, the Group Chairman, the Group Secretary and the Group Treasurer, and find that it is time usefully spent.

At some stage during the proceedings, it is desirable to offer light refreshments. This will offer the Group Scout Leader the opportunity to meet and become known to some of the new faces who may be present. It should be possible to leave the supervision of the tea pouring or organisation of the younger Members to other Leaders and supporters. The time of the Group Scout Leader and the Group Chairman is going to be better employed in meeting as many members of the Group Council as possible.

Conversation will often expose another facet of an individual and may reveal, for example, that in this person lies the expertise required to set up that outing for the Beaver Scout Colony. It may well be that some members of the Group Council have little time for active support, but it is fairly safe to assume that all members of the Group Council are broadly sympathetic to the Aim of The Scout Association. So, if the Cub Scout Pack is short of adult Leaders, it might be possible to arrange a rota of Group Council members to help Leaders out at weekly meetings on a temporary basis.

Such help is unlikely to be forthcoming voluntarily, but a personal request by the Group Scout Leader or Group Chairman will only be refused by the genuinely busy person. Indeed, how many of our adult Leaders become involved in just such a way?

Group Executive Committee

As previously mentioned, for day to day support, the Group Council, as such, would be far too cumbersome a body, so most of the routine work of administration and fund raising will be delegated to the Group Executive Committee. Every Scout Group must have an effective Executive Committee, otherwise the responsibilities fall heavily on the shoulders of the Leaders, but how many Scout Groups are 'top heavy' with Leaders?

Leaders should be working with the young Members, not attending meetings. The Group Scout Leader is the spokesperson for the Warranted Leaders and is the only one who must, of necessity, be present. Section Leaders are ex-officio, but do not have to be present.

The size of the Group Executive Committee will be determined by the size of the Group itself. It should be large enough to afford a fair representation of the whole Group and big enough to share the work–load so that it is not the same few who do all the work. However, it should also be small enough to enable effective discussion and decision making to take place.

After the Group Scout Leader, the Group Chairman, Group Secretary and the Group Treasurer, membership of the Group Executive Committee, as one would expect, will include the Assistant Group Scout Leader and Section Leaders who are ex–officio. In the case of a sponsored Group, the nominee of the Sponsoring Authority will also be a member.

There will also be a number of members nominated by the Group Scout Leader and these should include one parent from each Section of the Group. Further members may be elected by the Group Council at its Annual General Meeting but the number of these must not be more than the number nominated by the Group Scout Leader.

It is occasionally necessary for the Group Scout Leader, or Group Chairman, to remind a Group Executive Committee that their title does not give them executive power over the Group as a whole, but denotes only that they exist to carry out the wishes of the Group Council in supporting the work of the training Sections.

The functions of the Group Council and the Group Executive Committee are listed in ***Policy, Organisation and Rules*** and include financial management, public relations, property maintenance and assistance with adult recruitment.

The Group Executive Committee may find it more convenient to delegate some of its functions to small working groups or sub–Committees, for example, to oversee fund raising, property maintenance or other special projects. There is no need for members of these sub-Committees to be members of the Executive Committee – except for the fund raising sub-Committee – indeed, they may need not even be a member of the Group Council, but it is more usual that they will be.

For example a building sub-Committee might include a local builder with no more than a friendly interest in the Group. Every sub-Committee is responsible to the Group Executive Committee, and must make any recommendations through the Group Executive, but the Group Chairman should make sure that, whilst discussing the sub-Committee's reports, that they do not debate all the matters again, otherwise the sub-Committee will have been a waste of time.

Group Scouters Meeting

The Group's Scouters will discuss matters of concern to the training Sections in the Group Scouters' Meeting. Under the Chairmanship of the Group Scout Leader, all Leader Warrant holders in the Group, together with the Chairman of the Venture Scout Unit, will meet about every two months.

These meetings do not have to be as formal as meetings of the Group Council or Group Executive, but it is still a good idea to take minutes, or at least, notes of any decision made for circulation to interested parties.

Also, day to day problems will probably be handled by the Section Leaders concerned, the Group Scouters' Meeting may wish to take the opportunity to discuss individual Members of the Group who have, if any, problems of one sort or another.

The Group Scouters' Meeting also presents the means through which Scouters can make requests to the Group Executive Committee for expenditure beyond the individual Section budgets.

Perhaps the most important feature of the Group Scouters' Meeting is that of providing the opportunity of ensuring the progress and continuity of all Members in the Group. The Group Scouters Meeting is the place where all Scouters in the Group can combine their talents to determine that their Scout Group will operate as an efficient happy family unit.

Too many meetings?

A couple of thoughts about meetings...

First, there must be many Scout Leaders who think that what goes on at Troop night is of secondary importance to the number of committee meetings and the paper work to process. Perhaps we need to ask ourselves if every meeting is really necessary, and does everyone have to attend?

Second, everyone is happy when a meeting finishes earlier than expected, but they are equally put off by those meetings which drag on.

CHAPTER NINE

FINANCE MANAGEMENT AND FUND RAISING

One can imagine the little old person allocating, each week, a set portion of their fixed income to cover electricity bills and the like, and then setting each portion away in a jam jar.

Such prudent budgeting is very commendable and highly necessary when incomes are limited. Many people, however, apply this same 'jam jar' mentality to the role of the Group Treasurer, thinking that he or she is someone whose sole job is to collect the money and keep the accounts. It should be added, perhaps, that there are some Group Treasurers who take those thoughts literally and do their best to keep a tight rein on the accounts.

Again, whilst prudence is commendable, finances are there to be used for the benefit of Scouting in the Group and not to be retained in some Scrooge-like hoard.

Accurate accounts

Collecting money and keeping accurate accounts are essential elements of the Group Treasurer's role, but other things should be going on as well, such as advising on financial control, producing an annual budget, keeping tabs on (but not controlling) the accounting of Section funds, investing any funds not required immediately, supervising the administration of all property and equipment, ensuring there is adequate insurance cover for the Group, co-ordinating Group fund raising activities and generally watching over the entire financial life of the Scout Group.

It is quite obvious that the Scout Group Treasurer should have at least a good general knowledge of financial matters and certainly he or she should not be frightened by basic book–keeping, nor by the thought of handling money which may run into as much as thousands of pounds.

Some Scout Groups may be lucky enough to have a Treasurer who is professionally involved in the financial world, but most are likely to have an unqualified person with no specialist knowledge or expertise other than that acquired in the course of daily life. Either can do a perfectly good job as Group Treasurer provided, and this is important, that they are adequately briefed before taking up the appointment and given any necessary training.

Ideally, the responsibility for the briefing of any new Treasurer (and Secretary, come to that) will lie with the Group Chairman, although the Group Scout Leader should also be involved in this.

Even professionals will need such a briefing, because the finances of a Scout Group may well be run on different lines from, say, those of a major clearing bank – and those differences could well be quite important.

The District Treasurer may also be able to offer some help and advice, especially if the new Group Treasurer is not familiar with accounting practices and other points of procedure. It is essential that all Group Administrators should understand and accept their responsibilities.

Finance management

Every Scout Group is obliged to keep proper accounts and to have these audited annually. A copy of the audited accounts must be sent to the District Treasurer, not later than July 31, each year. The auditor is appointed at the Annual General Meeting and must be independent but not necessarily a qualified accountant. These audited accounts should include those funds administered by all the Sections.

Presentation of the audited accounts at the Annual General Meeting is often the one time of the year when the Group Treasurer emerges from the counting-house and all those attending the meeting will show appropriate pleasure or displeasure when the accounts reveal a surplus or deficit. Success or failure here often revolves around the degree of success in the drawing up of an accurate budget at the beginning of the year.

Alongside the budget, the Group Treasurer will probably have drawn up a cash flow forecast, indicating not only how much money is required for various purposes but also when. This allows for the facility to invest to the best advantage any funds not required immediately.

Section funds

Another potential minefield through which the Group Treasurer may have to venture is the Section funds. These will often be raised by charging Members a weekly, monthly or termly subscription. This should be set at a realistic figure to cover the week by week needs of of the Section – buying or replacing games equipment, handicraft materials and so on.

There is often a commendable desire by some Leaders to keep this subscription as low as possible and, of course, consideration must be taken of Members' economic circumstances. At the same time, however – human nature being what it is – we often really only appreciate what we have had to pay for. Little more than the cost of a packet of crisps, or less than the price of a can of cola, is unlikely to rate very highly in the minds of many young people.

There is another side to this as well. The purchasing power of low subscriptions is not going to be very supportive of innovative Scouting and programme quality.

The level of Sectional subscriptions is something which the Leaders may wish to discuss at Group Scouters' Meetings from time to time, but the final decision must be left, in each case, to those responsible for the administration of the Section.

If there is any element, however, of Sectional subscriptions being used for payment of annual Membership Subscriptions to Headquarters, County or District levies, this is a different matter. This portion of the subscriptions is clearly the Group Treasurer's responsibility and should be handled accordingly.

Similarly, any Membership Subscription which is covenanted should be passed to the Treasurer at the very earliest opportunity and paid into the Group account. (Note, the role of the Group Treasurer is dealt with more fully in **Supporting Scouting**, available from the Resource Centre, at Gilwell Park.)

Fund raising

Group Executive Committees are usually very good at assuming the role of fund raisers and are excellent at it too – often without much idea of what they want the money for.

Often, in their enthusiasm, they will involve Scouts and Scouters in these fund raising activities, though these are primarily the responsibility of the Group Administrators and the members of the Group Council. In some Scout Groups, it falls to the Group Executive Committee to handle. However it is organised, it should only be the Group Scout Leader who is directly involved in the planning of fund raising events.

Methods of fund raising will vary from one Scout Group to another, and from one place to another. An idea which may raise lots of money in one locality may be a complete failure elsewhere. Many well–established Groups will have a number of favourite ideas that have worked well in the past and continue to bring in a steady income, but it is always as well to be looking for a new angle, because, like fashion, what may be popular today is 'old hat' tomorrow. New ideas can often be gained from the pages of SCOUTING Magazine.

As an organisation, we are particularly good at raising money, especially for other charities. This is no doubt due, in part, to the principle that Scouts earn their funds, rather than holding out their hands for straight donations.

One last word on fund raising. It is all too easy to fall foul of the plethora of legal complexities that exist. Reference to ***Policy, Organisation and Rules***, may prove to be useful.

Alternatively, if you have any queries or require advice, contact the Legal Department, The Scout Association, Baden–Powell House, Queen's Gate, LONDON SW7 5JS.

CHAPTER TEN

MARKETING THE SCOUT GROUP

Go out and ask your friends, relatives or colleagues what they know most about household products advertised on television, and the chances are they will respond with the quip or jingle which they have seen and heard in those advertisements.

Ask the same people what they can tell you about Scouting and the chances are that many of them will not be able to go beyond 'knobbly knees and big hats', or maybe 'Dyb, Dyb, Dyb'.

They will have heard of 'Scouts', and many of them will have some vague notion that Scouting is 'a good thing', but they will not really know much more than that. The reason being not only do we not advertise on television, but our 'product' is not 'marketed' in the same aggressive fashion.

Is there a need?

Do we need to 'market' ourselves? With some 650,000 Members, The Scout Association is second only in size to our sister Movement The Guide Association, among voluntary youth organisations in the United Kingdom.

Gratifying though this may be, it gives no cause for complacency because it still only represents a tiny proportion of the available population for membership of the Movement and, in many places, our representation is nil.

For many of us, this offers a challenge – a vision of a growing Movement, reaching out to more young people, giving them a chance to enjoy our unique package of fun, adventure, community service, spiritual awareness and learning by doing.

Not everyone in Scouting shares this vision. Some people are quite content with their Beaver Scout Colony, Cub Scout Pack, Scout Troop or Venture Scout Unit, or they have enough to cope with as it is, or indeed they have never really given the matter much thought.

If the Scout Movement is to grow, it needs individuals who can motivate Scouters and Administrators, so that they will want to attract more young people.

How is this to be done?

The art of advertising is to make potential customers believe that they will be deprived if they do not buy the product. Advertisements pamper to vanity –'You're never alone with...' or 'All the best people buy...'

We do not live in an ideal world, therefore, we need to inspire a personal conviction in our Membership that, both for the sake of young people, and for the benefit of society in general, the Scout Movement must grow.

This can be achieved by enthusing Leaders into wanting to attract more members, and by recalling the Aims of the Movement as being directed at everyone and, by opening minds to the recognition that what is at stake is the well-being of future generations of young people in this country.

For the most inward-looking, there is the alternative argument that larger Sections and Groups have clear advantages including greater financial resources, more programme options, improved morale and so on. Success breeds success – who wants to board a sinking ship?

Some Leaders will respond to arguments on an idealistic plane – that Scouting is a healthy influence on young people and is therefore of benefit to all, for us to bring as many of them as possible into our ranks. This argument is especially valid in deprived areas,

whether inner city or remote and rural, where leisure pursuits are non-existent or of a less positive nature.

Plan of action

With any project, it is necessary to draw up a plan of action...

1. We need to decide exactly what we want to do. For example, are we going to address the 'loss' of Membership between the Sections?

2. We must define our objectives. For example, to improve the 'link' in order to reduce the 'loss' by say 20 per cent. It is important to set targets, but they must be realistic because unattainable targets will simply be ignored. High expectations do not necessarily lead to high achievement.

On the other hand, it is certain that low expectancy will have only one result – low achievement. The right balance is when realism is enhanced by healthy ambition.

3. We then set out our 'plan of action'. For example, how we propose to attain our target – weekend activity, joint meetings and so on. Progress should be monitored at least every six months.

Successes must be praised generously and good news communicated throughout the Scout Group, and maybe beyond. Approval and gratitude should be fostered and this should even touch upon those who are failing in their efforts – so long as there is an effort. One cannot beat a sense of team work so that all those involved feel that their labours are worthwhile and are appreciated.

Nobody can be asked to do anymore than his or her best, but without encouragement and enthusiasm for achievement, even when modest, it is all too easy not to bother trying.

4. It is important to be aware from the outset of the costs involved in any such project. They may be financial, such as providing refreshments for an event, or human, such as providing extra helping hands.

5. At the conclusion of the time period allocated for the exercise, it is necessary to look back and decide if the project was worthwhile. From this, we can then discuss and set any short–term or longer–term plans for the Group.

Actions speak louder than words

Any strategy can only happen if it is turned into action. We must not stop at number one. We must progress through the stages. It is not enough to analyse a particular problem, we must resolve to do something about it.

It is often said that it is attractive, adventurous and popular programmes which increases our Membership and that all we need to do is improve the quality of Scouting. This may be true to a point, but we cannot wait passively for youngsters to come flocking through the door, no more so than the manufacturer has merely to have this product placed on the shop shelves.

The manufacturer must advertise and market the product. Likewise, once our programme quality is right, we must let the potential customers know about it.

CHAPTER ELEVEN ADULT RECRUITMENT

Every Scout Group needs a manager to co-ordinate the activities of all the Sections, and to ensure the continuity and development of training.

This is usually the role of the Group Scout Leader. Even a single-Section Group is going to need someone to take on the responsibility of acting as a liaison between the Section, the Group Council, and between the various outside bodies.

Where there is no one available to take on the Group Scout Leader's role, the District Commissioner should appoint a person to fulfil the requirement until a permanent solution can be made.

All things to all people

The person who undertakes the duties and responsibilities of the Group Scout Leader must be a shoulder to cry on, as well as being the one to put a rocket behind the procrastinator. He or she will also be a peacemaker, an encourager, a co–ordinator, a teacher, a listener and an adviser. In other words, almost a paragon of virtue!

However, the Group Scout Leader may still fall short of the mark because he or she will also be human and, like the rest of us, can only do the best they can with the time and resources available. There is no doubt that it is a demanding job – possibly the most demanding job in Scouting if done to the full – and will draw heavily upon the energies of whoever takes it on.

Within the Scout Group there are likely to be a number of adults working for the Movement in different ways. Some are Leaders and Assistant Leaders or Helpers with the Sections, whilst there may also be Skills Instructors, who can be called upon for their specialist skills.

There are also the Group Administrators, including the Chairman, Treasurer and Secretary, who are all part of the team whose common purpose is to the benefit of the Members of the Group, Clearly, effective management of this team will be a keynote to the success of the Scout Group.

Shortage of Adults

Adult Leaders and Administrators form the backbone of the Scout

Movement and without the millions of hours they contribute to Scouting, voluntarily, every year, there would be no Scouting. Their skills and commitment are essential in providing the exciting and adventurous programmes that attract young people. It is not surprising then that a common cry is 'we cannot get enough Leaders'.

Most Scout Groups and Districts would welcome more adult help if only they could find the people, but there is no easy solutions to adult recruitment. However, a booklet entitled **Recruiting Adults: a practical guide**, has been produced based on extensive research and practical experience. It includes worksheets and sets out a step-by-step programme of recruitment to bring in all those potential adults who are just waiting to be asked.

Square pegs into round holes

If this sounds to good to be true, a survey undertaken on behalf of The Scout Association found that half the adult population are willing to support Scouting in some way. The secret is to find them and then invite them to do a job they will be happy to do.

That last sentence is the crux of the issue because the survey also determined that one stands a better chance of getting volunteers by the personal approach, seeking out those who have the skills to do something specific and to offer them a job that offers an exit after an agreed time.

Whose responsibility is it?

The requirements of each and every Scout Group will be different just as each person has different characteristics and abilities. The needs of the Section Leader may well be different from the needs of the Group Chairman. Similarly some volunteers will be able to offer assistance in helping to provide exciting and varied programmes for the Members in the Section while others may be better helping with fund–raising events or serving on committees.

Whose responsibility is it to recruit all these wonderful people? The answer is that no one has sole responsibility for recruitment. All adults in Scouting have a part to play in finding suitable people for the various appointments and tasks to be filled – often it results in being a team who does it.

Setting about the task

One of the best and most successful means of adult recruitment is the personal approach. An alternative method is to advertise for help. Which ever approach is taken, the key to success is to match up the right person to the right job.

If a manufacturer is going to advertise a product it is essential for the purchasing public to be told what they are going to get for their money. Similarly, the volunteer will need to know details of the actual job they will be fulfilling and the team must be clear as to what type of person is being sought. In order that this may be achieved satisfactorily, it will be necessary for the recruitment team to carefully think out beforehand what the actual job is and what skills are needed. It is only fair that the potential Leader or Administrator should understand the commitment they are about to undertake. In this day and age it is not good enough to fob people off with the 'only two hours a week' excuse.

Further questions will need to be answered giving details such as with whom they will be working, and what equipment or material will be available for the task. It will be helpful for the person to know who they can look to if they need help and, if possible, to set an end date to the job.

It is important to be able to show the recruit that it is not just a one-sided business that is being offered, and that some benefit will be derived from the exercise. Whilst Scouting is unlikely to help anyone to become a millionaire, it can make a big difference to health and happiness.

Who can we ask?

Once it is clear what is needed, the next task is for the team to look for people to match those requirements. It may be that a member of the team will know a suitable candidate who can be approached. By casting the net wide enough it is often possible to come up with a list of potential recruits. Look again at the adult Members already in the Scout Group, it could well be that there is someone possessing the necessary qualifications fulfilling a role for which it is easier to find a replacement.

At this stage it may be beneficial to arrange a meeting of interested parties, especially if the job is more than an occasional one. This will afford the time in a relaxed and comfortable setting to thoroughly explain the role and answer any questions. If the ground has been prepared well this will not be a formidable task.

A follow-up meeting may be necessary if further information is required or if it is necessary for other people, such as the District Commissioner, to be involved. If, at the end of all this the recruitment is unsuccessful, one should not be too despondent because there is no guaranteed method of adult recruitment, but if the groundwork has been thoroughly prepared the chances of success are improved.

Confidential enquiries

Although, as a general rule, the Scout Movement welcomes any offer of help from an adult with the Scouts' interest at heart, it must not be assumed that acceptance of such an offer is automatic. Before beginning work in a Scout Group, an enquiry procedure must be completed – unless the person has been introduced to the District by Headquarters in a written statement as to the person's suitability.

The procedure is as follows...

- The Group Scout Leader informs the District Commissioner and supplies the applicant's name, address, age and any claim to previous service in the Movement. This is done by completing Form **WE**.

- The District Secretary will then forward the enquiry to the Records Office, at Headquarters, and await a satisfactory reply (normally four or five days). This is not just 'red tape' but an essential part of the procedure if young people are to be protected from possible moral or physical danger.

- At the same time, it may also be appropriate to make local enquiries with other people in the area who know the candidate. If an adverse report is obtained locally, the District Commissioner or the District Secretary must be informed and Headquarters alerted. (A form is available to use for these local checks.)

Note – full details of adult recruitment will be found in **Recruiting Adults: a practical guide**, published by The Scout Association, obtainable from The Resource Centre, Gilwell Park. Further details of the confidential enquiry procedure, and other details of appointments procedure, may be found in ***Policy, Organisation and Rules***.

CHAPTER TWELVE

COMMUNICATIONS

Communications – possibly more hours have been spent within Scouting over this one word than any other, yet effective communications are essential to the success of any efficient organisation.

Just how effective are communications within your Scout Group? Does everyone who ought to know, get to know everything that they should know? There is no simple answer to our problem, but let us take a look at some types of communication that we use and their effectiveness.

Effective communication

To be effective, your communication also depends on other considerations. For example, it must appeal to the recipient. The method of approach must not be too aggressive or it may prove to be off–putting from the word go.

The layout of any notice or poster must catch the eye. As with the rest of us, you probably receive no end of 'junk mail' and, again, in common with the rest of us, most of that goes straight into the waste paper basket.

Sometimes, however, something catches your eye and you give the sheet of paper more than just that initial cursory glance. If you do that, regardless of whether you buy the advertised product or not, the layout artist has been successful. You must try to achieve the same effect.

Ensure that all the required information given in your communication is clear and stated in simple language.

The other essential element, and this is the one which all too often we fail on, is time. Your Communication must be put out in good time to allow for action to be taken and for any necessary follow–up. How often have you received information about a Scout function which could have proved interesting and/or useful only to find that it was last week or the closing date was yesterday?

If the information has to be passed on by hand to other recipients, this can take a very long time. In such instances, it is useful to give yourself time to make a follow-up.

Poor communication

There are many causes of poor communication...

Verbal instructions often fail if they are not delivered clearly, or if there is too much information given. Then again, if we are trying to tell a person something important, when half of their attention is elsewhere, say, those Cub Scouts in the corner making a lot of noise, we are clearly trying to impart information at the wrong time and/or in the wrong place. Sometimes the instructions given are lacking, or are not clear about what action the recipient has to take in following up the communication.

A badly produced circular or newsletter which is difficult or near impossible to read, has a crowded layout and is lacking in the essential information, such as who to reply to and so on, are common failings.

Closely allied to this is that unattractive notice on the board in an 'amateurish' hand, which has been up there so long that it is beginning to fade and curl at the edges – or else it has been placed so high that a step ladder is needed by anyone of average height to read it.

Again, failure to adopt positive steps for effective communication will result in poor communication – always make sure that all recipients are familiar with the system of circulation, that is, who is responsible for passing what on to whom, when and how.

Communications are not an 'optional extra' which we can choose to have or to reject, they are something that every Scout Group has – the only choice is whether they are good or bad. Furthermore, you will realise that it is more than one person's responsibility – effective communication calls for a team effort.

Each member of that team must know what is required of them and must be 'on the ball' regarding information and support material. If we are to get the best results from our communications we must understand and, most importantly, believe in what we are trying to do and why we are doing it.

CHAPTER THIRTEEN

A GROUP PROSPECTUS

Does the public in the area served by your Scout Group really know about what Scouting offers and is trying to achieve? Indeed, are all your parents or even the Group/District Executives well informed?

How do people view Scouts in your locality? A lively Group newsletter will undoubtedly help to inform interested parties, but have you considered producing a Group prospectus?

What is a prospectus?

A prospectus is simply a document that describes the main features of an organisation, in this case your Scout Group. It is aimed at the parents of potential new members, Leaders, sponsors and other benefactors, indeed anyone who may be interested to learn more about local Scouting.

Why write a prospectus?

A prospectus is a means of raising local awareness about your Scout Group. Although strictly intended merely to inform the public, a prospectus, if well written, can be a very useful marketing tool in all sorts of circumstances.

By painting an interesting picture about your Scout Group and stressing its value to the community, a prospectus can attract new members and Leaders as well as financial and material support.

To achieve this it will be most effective when used in conjunction with a recruitment drive or appeal for support.

Your prospectus will give more detailed information to interested parties, whose attention will first have been drawn by verbal contact, by a poster, letter or general leaflet about Scouting.

How do we produce a prospectus?

First you must write it! This must be undertaken by a capable writer, well informed about your Scout Group. Below you will find suggestions as to the contents of a prospectus. This can be no more than a set of guidelines – and there is no need to follow them exactly unless you wish to do so.

You will then need to have the text typed and illustrated, and the prospectus designed. Articles which appear from time to time in SCOUTING Magazine, and the **Artists' References** page and disks, in particular, are useful tools there for your benefit.

If you choose to use these, all that is asked is that you comply with the copyright of SCOUTING Magazine and include an acknowledgement as to your source, sending two copies of the final publication to the General Editor.

Have a good number printed and retain the print masters so that you can run off extra copies if needed. This should not be too expensive, but you should not sacrifice presentation for the sake of a few pounds.

The prospectus should be loose-bound, so that pages with out-dated information can easily be replaced.

Circulation

Ensure that you have an adequate supply on public occasions such as open evenings and on stalls at fund raising events. Enclose a copy with letters you write asking for support or sponsorship, and personally hand a copy to anyone you are requesting help from.

You should also send a prospectus to all existing supporters, parents, your local authority, local celebrities and persons of influence such as Councillors and the business community. Members of Parliament are often very anxious to learn of what is happening in their constituency and this is a very good vehicle for informing them.

Prospectus synopsis

This is an outline of a suitable prospectus, adapt it to your own needs and circumstances as you see fit.

Introduction

Tell the reader in a few sentences what the prospectus is, and why you have published it.

What is Scouting?

Give a brief history of the Scout Movement and describe its Aim and Method. Include all the fundamentals such as the Scout Promise and the Scout Law, uniform, structure and Membership.

There is little point in writing about the progressive training scheme and activities here, as these will emerge from your review of the Scout Group which follows.

Your Scout Group

Begin with a short history of the Scout Group, but be careful not to duplicate any information already given in the prospectus. Then go on to relate the Sectional training programme, activities and major events of each Section in turn with a note about any future plans the Group may have.

Keep to the highlights – you will bore your readers if you detail everything – you should aim simply to give a flavour of the life of the Scout Group concerned.

Introduce your Leadership team by name to give the prospectus a human touch. You can perhaps afford to be a little light-hearted in your description of each Scouter – but don't overdo it!

Next, you should go on to say what facilities and equipment you have. It may be useful to include your previous year's accounts – or a summary of them – in the prospectus with a covering note from the Group Treasurer.

The Scout District

Tell the reader which Scout District your Group lies in, with a few details about its function, other Scout Groups in the District and various District events.

Mention the District Scout Fellowship if there is one. A one-sentence reference to the County may be worth adding too.

Finally...

Producing a prospectus may well be beyond the means of your Scout Group. If so, why not consider publishing a joint document with a neighbouring Group, or even a District prospectus?

Make sure the prospectus has a contact name, address and telephone number. If you do produce a prospectus, review the project after a predetermined interval to judge what impact it has made in your locality, so that your experience may be shared with others for their benefit too.

CHAPTER FOURTEEN

MEETING PLACES

Anyone who has had to run a Scout Group in a place of worship's hall or school, has experienced some of those problems which crop up from time to time such as, what can be done to occupy the Cub Scout Pack on a wet February night when the school is closed for half-term?

Who is going to explain to the religious leader yet another broken window, or what to do with the wet canvas brought back from camp? Can they not be forgiven for envying that nearby Group with a place of its own?

Utopia...

A Scout Group that has its own headquarters has a place in which to store its equipment. Meetings can continue during the school holidays, pictures and charts can be put up on walls and the door can be closed on the remnants of the jumble sale, and the clearing-up done tomorrow – what bliss!

...or is it?

Compare this with those 'lucky' Scout Groups which meet in a place of a worship's hall or school – they may enjoy the benefits of sponsorship, lighting and heating at an economical rental. Many can also arrange for a lockable 'Scout cupboard' or garage on the premises, or are lucky enough to enjoy the hospitality of a friendly caretaker. Which is the lucky one?

Even assuming that the Scout Group has been on that plot of land since the year dot, there will still be problems – there will be council tax demands, insurance premiums, electricity and heating bills, as well as the cost of regular maintenance and repairs.

Must have somewhere

The desire to build your own Group headquarters is a big step and should not be taken lightly. A great deal of thought and thorough investigation should be undertaken, including seeking advice from Scout Headquarters at Baden-Powell House, before making any decisions.

Anyone who does embark on such a project, whether they have the freehold and are building on land which they own, or building on land which is rented under long-term leasehold agreement, will soon find they are entering a minefield of complex procedures through which they need the help which is available from Headquarters.

A Scout Group **cannot** own land or buildings in its own name, therefore, any Group which has its own headquarters must appoint Trustees to hold the property on trust for the Scout Group.

Local Trustees can be appointed but with today's mobile society, this may cause problems if one of the Trustees moves away from the immediate area. Many Groups ask The Scout Association Trust Corporation (set up by the Association for this very purpose) to act as Trustee. The legal details of the Trusteeship are quite complicated but, once again, further details can be obtained from Baden–Powell House, in London.

Charity Commissioners

Any Scout Group in England or Wales which occupies land with or without buildings on it, must be registered as a separate charity by the Charity Commissioners. In the case of a Scout Group which has placed Trusteeship with the Scout Association Trust Corporation, this application will be made on its behalf by the Corporation.

The Group Secretary must ensure that all the obligations which are imposed by the Charity Commissioners are fulfilled.

Since January 1, 1993, it has been a requirement that every registered charity with an income of £5,000 or more, in the last financial year, must display its charitable status on all documentation, such as cheques, invoices, receipts and so on. It is recommended that every Scout Group which is registered, and all Groups are not required to be registered, when ordering printed stationery and cheque books, should print 'Charity Registration Number...' on all such items.

Whether in your own headquarters, or in rented accommodation, Scout Groups must be properly accommodated and equipped in order to carry out their training programmes. This responsibility falls upon the Administrators of the Group who must concern themselves with all legal requirements relevant to the ownership of all property and equipment or to the hiring of premises.

Maintenance and use

Like any other owner–occupier, a Scout Group with its own headquarters faces a number of overheads. Maintenance must be carried out to keep the property in good condition, and it must be redecorated from time to time.

Scout Groups registered with the Charity Commissioners have been able to obtain financial relief at the discretion of the local authority, to which application for details should be made.

Any Scout Group which has its own buildings must also clearly make adequate insurance arrangements to cover the cost of any rebuilding at current prices. The sum insured will need to include an allowance for costs, such as architects' fees, planning procedures and site clearance prior to rebuilding, as well as rebuilding itself, and must be reviewed annually to ensure that it is still appropriate.

Many building insurance policies, including the 'Scout Property and Equipment Insurance Policy', available through the Insurance Department at Lancing, include an 'escalation clause' which automatically adjusts the insured value in line with any general change in property values, but it is still the Group's own responsibility to ensure that the cover is adequate.

A close eye should be kept on land and building prices because if they start to rise again, as they frequently have done until recent years, a Scout Group which lets the insured value of its headquarters become even 12 months out-of-date could face a loss of several thousand pounds should anything go wrong. This sort of risk is simply not acceptable, and the Group Treasurer must ensure that the Group headquarters, along with all other Group property and equipment is fully covered by insurance at all times.

Almost every Group will possess some items of equipment – tents, ropes, cooking gear and so on, and this, too, must be adequately insured. It may be possible to include equipment in the same policy as the buildings – the special Scout policy already referred to offers this facility – but the cover should include risks incurred while away from the headquarters (for example, in camp or in transit).

Groups should also consider insuring at least the main items on a 'full replacement cost' basis, so that if a ten-year-old tent burns down, the insurance payment will be enough to provide another tent, rather than being reduced by ten years' worth of depreciation.

It is important to remember that the insurers will also want assurance that the Scout Group takes all possible precautions to make its property secure. Effective locks and secure windows – as well as the building itself being sound – are obvious requirements, and the local crime Prevention Officer will always be happy to give advice on the appropriate steps to take.

For example, if the building is an old wooden structure in an unlit back ally with some broken windows, rotting door, window frames and a lock which even a Cub Scout could open with a penknife, then it stands to reason that any reputable insurance company will not want the business!

If the Group has its own minibus or other transport, then this too must be adequately covered by the motor insurance necessary to comply with the requirements of the Road Traffic Act of 1988, in respect of third party and passenger liability risks. Again, information on the use of minibuses is available from the Legal Department at Headquarters.

Preferably, the vehicle should be insured on a fully comprehensive basis, or a least be insured against accidental damage, fire and theft. Similarly, appropriate marine and aviation insurance must be arranged for any Scout Group which owns boats (including canoes) or aircraft of any description, to cover the risks of loss or damage to such items.

Whilst it may be worth 'shopping around', especially for the motor insurance policy, it should be remembered that many companies impose restrictions on the minimum age or experience of drivers. However, these policies, too, can be arranged through the Association's Insurance Department, Lancing.

The premiums payable on policies arranged in this way compare favourably with those on the open market and, there is the advantage that the Insurance Department policies are specially geared to the needs of Scout Groups.

Now that we have our headquarters built and insured, the more that it is used, the more economically viable it becomes. Many Scout headquarters are used only in the evenings and at weekends, but stand idle all day.

Making the building available at this time to the local 'over-sixties' day centre or a play-group provides additional income. The latter, however, has its own legal requirements for storing equipment, thus it is as well to clarify their demands before undertaking any contracts.

Clearly, there must be someone appointed by the Group Executive Committee to handle bookings and so avoid clashes. It should be remembered, however, that if the Scout Group derives any substantial income from letting, particularly from non-charitable bodies, and/or if the turnover of the Group is great, it may affect eligibility for local tax relief, greater insurance or render it liable for Value Added Tax.

CHAPTER FIFTEEN

EQUIPMENT

In the last chapter we looked at the ins and outs of building and owning your own headquarters. We now move on to look into a few of the pros and cons of...

Group equipment

Many of the minor items of equipment that are used by a Scout Group, for example, knotting ropes, books, footballs and so on, will belong to each individual Section of the Group rather than to the Group as a whole.

This distinction should be respected and the Cub Scouts should not use the Troop's maps without first asking, and vice-versa. Hopefully, in true Scouting spirit, such permission will be readily given, but respect for someone else's property is fundamental to the Scout Law. If such equipment is stored in identified cupboards or boxes rather than just bundled collectively in one room, respect of ownership will be easier to achieve.

Larger equipment

Most Groups, however, will have many larger items of equipment, such as camping gear, which are owned collectively by the Group, rather than just by one Section. A scheme is required for the proper storage and upkeep of this equipment and it may well be desirable to appoint a Group Quartermaster.

This equipment officer will not be expected to handle all maintenance of the equipment alone. If the Scout Troop for instance, takes tents away for a weekend camp, then it is the Scout Troop which must see that those tents are clean and properly packed down afterwards. But the Quartermaster has the responsibility of ensuring the equipment is properly stored, that it is repaired or replaced when wear and tear take their toll, that it is made available when it is needed and, that equipment is properly booked out and in again when it is returned.

What is ours?

In the case of a Sponsored Group, it is essential that there is a written and clearly understood agreement as to which property and equipment belongs to the Scout Group and which to the Sponsoring Authority.

The Group Executive and Sponsoring Authority should have come to such an agreement when the Scout Group was first registered, and the agreement must be reviewed annually to take account of any new acquisitions or disposals that have occurred.

There must be an agreement, too, as to how the Group's funds are to be disposed of in the event of the Group's closure. A copy of the agreement must be lodged with the District Secretary. A model agreement form is available from Headquarters.

Budget wisely

It should be remembered that most equipment is expendable and will need replacing at some time or another.

The Quartermaster will need to bear this in mind and advise the Group Executive, which should have been prudently allowing for equipment replacement in its annual budget, so that the necessary replacement of an expensive piece of equipment does not come as too nasty a shock.

Group transport

It has already been said that a Scout Group may have its own transport, in which case, in addition to the insurance requirement already covered, there must be provision made in the budget for proper maintenance and other costs incurred, such as road tax and fuel.

Not only will it be necessary to keep such a vehicle in first class condition because it is carrying people, the image created by its appearance will reflect for the good or otherwise upon the Movement as a whole.

CHAPTER SIXTEEN

THE SCOUT DISTRICT

Everyone, from the youngest Beaver Scout to the adult Leader, who joins the Scout Movement by making the appropriate Promise will thus become entitled to wear the World Membership Badge.

The chances are they will also be welcomed into the world-wide family of Scouts. Alas, in far too many Scout Groups, that is where the world-wide family stops!

It's all a question of relativity

The odds are that whilst the Members of the Scout Group can relate the fortunes of the local football team, to mention the Scout Group down the road is to involve the arch-enemies. Questioning will often reveal that more is known about extra-terrestrial bodies than that Group.

Group loyalty is commendable and to be encouraged but all too often it can lead to a Group being very parochial.

That neighbouring Scout Group is as much a part of the world-wide family of Scouts as anyone else, because every Group in a specified area is part of a Scout District – the size and composition of which will depend upon it's location.

For example, a large town or city may have as many as ten Groups within two square kilometres or so. On the other hand, there are some Scout Districts in this country which cover a larger area than a medium-sized shire county, with just a few Groups separated by as many kilometres. Whilst two such Districts cannot operate in the same way, their fundamental function is the same.

Boundaries

Policy, Organisation and Rules states 'The purpose of the Scout District within the structure of the Scout Movement is to provide leadership, advice and support for Scout Groups in an area the boundaries of which will correspond, in so far as possible, with those of the local authorities.

'County headquarters, in consultation with County and District Commissioners, decide where these boundaries are to be drawn, guided by the principle that the District Commissioner should be able to be in touch with all the Groups and all the Members of the Movement in the area and bearing in mind the local boundaries established by The Guide Association. On occasion, it may be necessary to adapt boundaries to suit these various needs'.

Anyone involved in the administration of the Scout District will know how true that last sentence is!

The District supports the Groups within its boundaries, but it is within the Scout Group that the Aim of the Association is fulfilled.

Supporting the District

Leading the District is the District Commissioner, who is supported by the District Team, comprising of (in many cases) a Deputy District Commissioner and Assistant District Commissioners for the various Sections, for Leader Training, or for other such responsibilities as the District Commissioner may consider necessary. Some Districts also have District Leaders, whose responsibilities will lie within a particular Section.

The Assistant District Commissioner is required to complete Commissioner training, whereas the requirement for a District Scouter is to complete training as for a Section Leader. If the District has formed a District Scoutlink Club, this should also be represented on the District Team.

Most Districts will also have a District Scout Fellowship and it is a wise District Commissioner who ensures that this is so, for the support and service they can give to the District is endless. Membership of the Scout Fellowship is open to anyone over the age of eighteen years (there is no upper limit) who supports the Aim and Method of The Scout Association.

Some members of the Scout Fellowship may be Venture Scouts or Warranted Leaders (who should give priority to their Unit or Group), but others are often simply interested and sympathetic members of the public who wish to support Scouting. Scout Fellowship membership may also consist of former Members of the Movement who are no longer able to commit themselves to any specific appointment nor to one particular Group.

The form of support given by the Scout Fellowship will vary from one District to another in accordance with the needs of the District and the strength of membership of the Scout Fellowship.

Some Scout Fellowships provide a service team to look after the District camp site, run special fund raising activities, or organise an 'emergency Scouter service' to provide temporary Leaders for Sections whose own Leaders are ill or on Holiday. There is usually a wealth of experience lurking in the Fellowship – it may even supply the support team for a major District activity.

In addition, most Scout Fellowships also arrange social activities for their own members and for the adult members of the District. Liaison with the District Scout Fellowship is the responsibility of the Group Scout Leader and the Group Chairman.

Help, support and administration

The District will have a District Scout Council and a District Executive Committee, with a Chairman, Secretary and Treasurer whose roles are very similar to those of the corresponding Group Administrators.

Many Districts will have an Appointments Secretary to look after the processing of Leader Warrants and most will have a Badge Secretary to administer the sale and supply of badges. Some Districts will also run their own Scout shop and have someone responsible for this valuable service to the District – often another function of the Scout Fellowship.

There may also be District Advisers for such matters as water activities, mountaineering, public relations and so on – these people are appointed by the District but are available to help and advise Groups and Sections as necessary.

The Assistant District Commissioners and other members of the District Team are available to help and support Groups in a variety of ways. Sometimes the support is given on an individual basis – any Scouter in need of advice is quite free to contact the appropriate Assistant District Commissioner or District Leader, and Group Administrators have a similar 'hot line' to their District counterparts.

The Assistant District Commissioners for the various Sections will probably have a visiting programme of some kind, calling in on the Section meetings every few months to pass on information, to offer support as necessary, or alternatively to collect good ideas to pass on to other less successful Sections.

The District Team should meet regularly and most Districts will include Group Scout Leaders as members of this meeting. One of the purposes of this meeting is to plan the programme of visits to Scout Groups and local Venture Scout Units and to give support and encouragement to the Leaders. So any Section which is not visited by a member of the District Team at least once a year, has good reason to complain that the Team is failing in its responsibilities.

Generally, however, the Scout Groups are supported collectively by the District. Most Districts hold a regular District Scouter's meeting to inform Leaders of and, to help plan District events, maybe discuss problems, or to learn new games and Scouting skills. These meetings also afford the opportunity for individuals to bounce ideas off their colleagues. In small Districts, these meetings may include all Scouters in the District, whereas in the larger Districts they may specialise on membership from those attached to one particular Section.

It has already been stressed that the District is in existence to support the Scout Groups, and it is only right that the Group should look to the District for this support, but many Districts find it frustrating because they can only give as much support as the Group is ready to receive. All too often the Groups who complain loudly about lack of District help are the same Groups who fail to send representatives to the District Scouter's meetings, are absent from District events and activities, and who look upon the Commissioners' visits as an unwelcome intrusion of their meeting.

The District is there to offer support, but it is up to the Scout Group to accept that support graciously, after all it is, itself, part of the District.

CHAPTER SEVENTEEN

SCOUT COUNTY AND HEADQUARTERS SERVICES

'They', it has been said for many years, are the little people who are locked away and brought out by the advertising agencies to make their products look bigger and better than their competitors.

'They' are also a special breed of people whom we all encounter at some time or another. Faceless and nameless 'they' are usually to blame for all trials and tribulations and, may come in the form of managers, officials, politicians and so on. In Scouting 'they' are synonymous with County and Headquarters personnel.

The County (Area)

The organisation of the Scout County (or area in Scotland and Wales) is basically comparable with the Scout District. Most Scout Counties follow the same boundaries as the corresponding local government counties, albeit some (including the Scottish Areas) are sub–divisions and a few still follow the 'old' boundaries established before the last Government revision.

Each County will have a County Commissioner, maybe a Deputy County Commissioner, but certainly there will be Assistant County Commissioners and Advisers with specific responsibilities. As in the District, there will be a team of Administrators who will mostly be volunteers, appointed in the same way as any other Scouters, but increasingly at County level, an Office is being established to deal with some of the administrative work or fund raising and these will be staffed with one or two full or part-time employees of the County Scout Council.

As a general rule, the County supports the District rather than the Scout Groups directly, although, occasionally, it may organise some events for Scouters or for the Membership as a whole.

The size of the County, both numerically and geographically, will dictate the degree of contact between the County Team and the Scout Groups.

Headquarters services

The arrangement of the Headquarters of The Scout Association is slightly different from County or District level. The services offered are available to help Leaders and Administrators by supporting the provision of better Scouting.

The nominal Leader of the Association is the Chief Scout, but the day to day business is in the hands of the Chief Executive Commissioner. The Chief Scout thus leads the voluntary sector and the Chief Executive Commissioner heads up the staff of the Association.

Decision making

Decision making is the responsibility of the Committee of the Council (the equivalent to a Board of Directors) which comprises of ex-officio, elected and co-opted members from the Council of The Scout Association. Apart from the Chief Executive Commissioner and invited staff members, all members of the Committee of the Council are volunteers from the Movement.

The members of the Committee of the Council are people who have an active role at various levels within the Movement and who are representative of the voluntary Movement nationally. They have to make their decisions at a national level utilising their own local Scouting experience and knowledge to form a greater and more comprehensive information base from which to work.

The decisions are taken to encompass the overall needs of the Movement with local decisions, within policy, being dealt with by those closer to the situation, who will have a better understanding of the local circumstances.

The Committee of the Council is supported by the Executive Committee and four sub-Committees: Programme and Training; Community Development; General Purposes; and Finance, whose functions are clear from their titles.

There is also a Chief Scout's Committee which offers access to the Committee of the Council by Group Scout Leaders, District Commissioners and County Commissioners through the Chief Commissioners. In addition there are nine National Teams – Beaver Scouts, Cub Scouts, Scouts, Venture Scouts, Activities, Adult Support, Chaplaincy, International and Special Needs, and Headquarters Boards and Task Forces which feed into the four sub-Committees. Volunteer Members of the Movement from all over the United Kingdom represent adults on these Teams and make recommendations to the sub-Committees of the Association.

Headquarters Departments

Headquarters Departments provide the services which are essential if the Chief Scout, the Committee of the Council, its sub-Committees, National Teams and Headquarters Boards are to guide the Movement effectively. The Committee of the Council is the body that formulates the policies. The task of Headquarters is to implement and offer support for its decisions.

Baden–Powell House

- **The Chief Executive Commissioner** is responsible for all the work of Headquarters, wherever situated, and for implementation of the policies of the Committee of the Council.

- **The Secretary of The Scout Association** is also Secretary to the Committee of the Council and provides support for County Secretaries. The Secretary advises the Movement on ***Policy, Organisation and Rules*** and is responsible for the Legal Department, Trust Corporation, Personnel, Archives, Organising Department and the Records Office, at Lancing.

- **The Director of Finance and Marketing** is responsible for overall control of all finances, Estates and Property, and the Marketing and Trading operations of the Association.

- **The Finance and Marketing Department** supervises the cash flow of the Association by monitoring the receipt of all monies from Membership Subscription, legacies, donations, fund raising, advises on and issues Covenant Forms and so on. It is also responsible for the development and implementation of national fund raising.

  The Department is additionally responsible for the co-ordination of approaches to Government departments, sponsors, donors and other potential supporters. Advises Counties and Districts on financial matters.

- **Personnel** is responsible for all staff matters relating to Headquarters, (excluding Scout Shops Limited), in particular staff recruitment, development and training, employee relations, health and safety and salary administration. Personnel provides advice to managers, and Scout Counties and Districts on employment of paid staff and to the Members of the Movement on employment issues.

- **The Legal Department** provides legal advice to Headquarters, Groups, Counties and Districts. It also administers The Scout Association Trust Corporation, which any Scout Council may appoint to act as Custodian Trustee of Freehold or Leasehold property or investments and keeps a watch on new legislation.

  The Department is not staffed to act as solicitor to the Scout Council, but advises when and how professional solicitors' advice should be sought.

- **Organising Department** organises events such as the National Scout Service at Windsor, and national conferences. The Department also provides support for the Scout Fellowship.

- **Community Development Department** supports the Counties and Districts in development to enable more young people to gain from the benefits of Scouting. Staff provide information and guidance, produce publications on expansion, re-organisation and innovative methods of Scouting, processes applications to the Scout Foundation for this work and also offers fieldwork.

  Scoutreach and the Ethnic Communities Development Programmes support the regeneration or establishment of Scout Groups in isolated rural and inner city areas. Liaison with organisations from the many ethnic minority communities is undertaken at national level.

  The Community Action Programme is about meeting the needs of young people through making the Movement's knowledge, experience and skill available to those not attracted to Membership.

  Community Relations maintains contact with other national bodies to alert Scouting to changing needs.

- **Public Relations Department** links the Movement to the media and vice versa. It also offers advice on good public relations techniques and practical help in dealing with problems. The Public Relations Department publishes **Talking Points**, a digest of news and information – it also provides support for national events, exhibitions and promotions.

- **Design Studio** supports all Departments in Headquarters but in particular Public Relations.

- **Editorial Department** publishes SCOUTING Magazine. It also commissions and produces training handbooks and other publications. The Publications Section collaborates with independent publishers and printers in book production and promotion.

- **Archives** maintains records, documents and other historical reference material covering the development of the Movement. Archives gives advice and information on Scouting history.

- **International Department** promotes contacts between Scouts of the United Kingdom and Members of overseas Associations, through advice to Assistant County Commissioners (International) and Leaders. The International Department encourages and organises international opportunities, supports the Association's 16 overseas Branches and 43 British Scout Groups abroad.

- **Chief Scout's Office** provides a central point of contact with the Chief Scout. The Office co-ordinates the Chief Scout's diary of visits and other engagements.

- **Baden-Powell House Hostel** provides residential and catering facilities for Members of The Scout Association, The Guide Association and their families. Baden-Powell House Conference Centre provides facilities for conferences, seminars, training courses and social events. Visits in the capital can also be arranged.

- **Field Commissioner Service** provides 16 members throughout England and Wales to advise and assist County Commissioners in the development of Scouting. A seventeenth Field Commissioner works with British Scouts based in Western Europe.

Gilwell Park

- **Programme and Training** monitors and develops the programmes of the four training Sections. It also devises training for Leaders, Commissioners, tutors and trainers, and co-ordinates the work of the nine National Teams (although only eight actually receive support from Programme and Training), maintains and monitors records of aspects of adult training. Programme and Training provides support to adults (from recruitment to retirement), Members and Leaders in outdoor pursuits, creative activities, technology, and supports and encourages spiritual development.

- **The Resource Centre** is the mail order outlet for resource material, information sheets, promotional posters and training material.

- **Estates Department** is responsible for the management, upkeep and development of the Association's properties and Conference facilities throughout the country including Baden-Powell House, Gilwell Park Camp site and Hawkhirst Adventure Camp.

Lancing

- **The Records Office** maintains a record of Appointments and Group Registrations, issues awards and collates statistics from the Annual Census returns.

- **Accounts Department** (There are also Accounts Departments at Baden-Powell House and Gilwell Park.) administers the Short Term Investment Service, operates the Scout and Guide Trust Fund for longer term investments and prepares the Association's Annual Accounts.

- **The Insurance Department** administers policies which provide benefits for Members where injury or illness occurs during Scouting activities. It also arranges supplementary insurance cover and gives advice on insurance matters generally.

- **Scout Shops Limited** is an independent company which contributes its entire net profit to The Scout Association. Scout Shops Ltd. supplies District Shops and appointed agents with goods and provides a Direct Mail Order service. The company also manages a chain of 24 Camping and Outdoor Centres to improve profitability through sales of tents, camping equipment and leisure wear to the public and offers a local service for Members.

CHAPTER EIGHTEEN

THE INTERNATIONAL DIMENSION

It was a great day for Scouting when the Iron Curtain was rolled away because it now means that Scouts are to be found in almost every country in the world, with only a few exceptions. We can now truly claim that we are Members of a world-wide family.

With more frontier restrictions disappearing and with many towns twinned with communities overseas, Scouts are presented with more opportunities than ever before to bring an international flavour into their programmes.

Historical development

Within a short time of Baden-Powell's experimental camp at Brownsea Island, in 1907, and the subsequent popularity of his book **Scouting for Boys**, Scout Movements began to develop around the world. By 1909, Scouting was established in many of the old British Empire countries. When Baden-Powell visited the United States in 1910, he found Scouting already flourishing there.

The spread continued and one of the results of the first World Scout Jamboree at Olympia, London, in 1920, was the creation of the Boy Scouts International Conference. All 31 nations represented at Olympia were founder members. A Bureau was established at 25 Buckingham Palace Road and the then United Kingdom International Commissioner, Hubert S. Martin, was appointed as Honorary Director.

The Boy Scouts International Conference was later superseded by the World Scout Conference which today, has 141 national Scout Associations or Federations in its membership. Total membership is now over 25 million in over 200 countries and territories.

The World Organisation of the Scout Movement

The World Organisation of the Scout Movement (WOSM) consists of the World Scout Conference, comprising of national Scout organisations and Federations, which meets triennially with different countries acting as host on each occasion. The meetings last about one week and convene to receive reports of progress from plans made at the previous meeting, and to review and lay plans for future developments in World Scouting.

The World Scout Committee

This consists of 12 people from 12 countries. They serve no national interests but only the interests of World Scouting. Committee members serve a maximum of six years, one third of which retire at each World Conference.

Because membership is global, meetings are kept to a minimum and much of the work is carried on through correspondence. There is a Steering Group of four Committee members who can more easily meet and take action. The World Scout Committee periodically forms sub-Committees, task forces and groups. The Committee of the Council of the United Kingdom Scout Association authorises members to serve on these.

The World Scout Bureau

This is located in Geneva and consists of the Secretary-General, some ten Directors, Assistants and supporting clerical staff. Major departments deal with Support Services, Community Development, Adult Resources and Public Relations.

Regions

The Scout 'world' is divided into five Regions, each with its own Bureau and supporting staff. The United Kingdom Scout Association is, naturally, primarily involved as a member of the European Region but has branches in some other Regions as well.

The European Region works closely with the Europe Region's WAGGGS (World Association of Girl Guides and Girl Scouts) and they hold a joint conference every three years. The European office, based in Brussels, is staffed by Scout and Guide Executives, of whom five serve this Scout Region, which comprises of 62 Associations with 1.8 million Members. The United Kingdom Scout Association makes an important contribution to the work and programme of the Region and, apart from Members who serve on the main Committees, a number of professional staff and volunteers also serve in specialised fields as needs arise.

The Region is also actively engaged in the work of other bodies, the European Youth Foundation and the European Youth Centre being amongst them.

IFOFSAG

The International Fellowship of Former Scouts and Guides (IFOFSAG) was founded in 1953 for the benefit of an adult movement based on Scout and Guide ideals and not limited to former Members of the Scout and Guide Movement. Thus, anyone over the age of eighteen who joins the Scout Fellowship and makes the Scout Promise becomes automatically a member of IFOFSAG.

The International Fellowship has the approval of the World Conference of the World Organisation of the Scout Movement and the World Conference of the World Association of Girl Guides and Girl Scouts. Membership of the International Fellowship is co-ordinated through one of the little known links between The Scout Association and The Guide Association – the Joint National Committee of the United Kingdom Scout Fellowship and Trefoil Guild. This Committee is made up of representatives from both the Scout Fellowship and the Trefoil Guild, which is the non-uniformed adult section of The Guide Association.

CHAPTER NINETEEN

PERSONAL TRAINING

At this point, especially if you are fairly new to the 'game' of Scouting, you may well be wondering how on earth anyone can be expected to cope with running a Scout Group.

Have no fear. The Scout Association has an excellent Training Programme for all its 'managers' (Group Scout Leaders, Commissioners and Administrators), so you will not be left to flounder. Indeed, The Scout Association won a National Training Award in 1991 for the excellence of this Modular Based Training Programme.

Functionality

The function of the Group Scout Leader, Commissioner and Administrator may differ, but they all have one thing in common - they all support the Section Leaders, who provide Scouting for young people.

The training for an adult in a management role in Scouting is, of necessity, different from the training of Leaders working with young people.

Group Scout Leaders and Commissioners will usually bring with them a maturity and a wide range of experience, maybe from industry or commerce and will have acquired skills and techniques relevant to sharing in this management role. They also have many skills developed in other social and family activities. The scheme of training recognises this prior learning, as well as taking into account the needs of the Movement and allows each participant to plan his/her training with the help of an experienced Leader. Administrators can also take advantage of all or part of the scheme.

The job description

Before attending any training, the newly appointed person will attend a 'profile interview' usually with the 'line manager', that is, the person who appoints them and to whom they will be responsible. For example, the line manager of the new Scout Group Leader will be the District Commissioner. The interview will usually consist of an evening or two in a relaxed informal setting.

Any appointment that someone takes up in Scouting needs to be accompanied by a job description and this will have been agreed between the person taking that job and their line manager at the profile interview. (In the examples that follow, the role of the Group Scout Leader will be taken but similar requirements apply to the other appointments of Commissioners and Administrators. Full details together with a comparison between appointments will be found in the Association's publication **Support for training: guidance and information – Group Scout Leaders, Commissioners and Administrators**.

Job title: Group Scout Leader

Responsible to...

(line manager)

District Commissioner

Responsible for...

Assistant Group Scout Leader

Section Leaders and Assistant Leaders

Group Chairman

Helpers and Skills Instructors

Advisers

Section Members

Main contacts (External)

Parents and members of the Group Council

The Guide Association locally

Other Youth Organisations

Leaders in the community

Local support organisations, for example, Service Clubs

Local civic and religious bodies

Neighbours of the Group headquarters

Main contacts (Internal)

Group Executive Committee

Leaders

Section Leaders

Other Group Scout Leaders

Assistant District Commissioners

District Secretary and Treasurer

Unit Executive

District Scouters and advisers

District Public Relations Officers

Sponsoring Authority (if applicable)

Job summary

To ensure the effective operation of the Scout Group and the development of Scouting within the Group in accordance with the Aim, Method and Policies of The Scout Association.

Main task summary

In the table (highlighting training units) which follows, it is suggested that the headings are used as a framework for deciding the main tasks for the job description. Fully detailed ideas of the main tasks will be found in **Support for training: guidance and information – Group Scout Leaders, Commissioners and Administrators**.

Unit 1 Aim and method	Responsible for ensuring that the Aim, Method, Policy and Training Scheme is carried out in the Group.
Unit 2 Support Leaders	Responsible for supporting all Leaders in the Group carrying out their tasks.
Unit 3 Safety	Responsible for safety in the Group.
Unit 4 Administration	Responsible for ensuring effective administration in the Group.
Unit 5 Working with a team of adults	Maintain a team of adults working together and with others.
Unit 6 Managing	Responsible for effective management of the Group.
Unit 7 Training duties	Responsible for the training and development of all Leaders and Administrators in the Group.
Unit 8 Local community	Responsible for adequate and proper representation of Scouting in the local community.
Unit 9 Public relations	Responsible for taking local Scouting to the public.
Unit 10 Development	Responsible for managing the development of Scouting in the Group's area including recruitment.
Unit 11 Special Needs/ International	Responsible for promoting Headquarters Policy and procedures in these topics.

The Training Units

The training provided for the Group Scout Leaders, Commissioners and Administrators is in a series of modules known as units. Most units cover one main area but the area itself will usually consist of several topics and follow the headings listed in the foregoing table.
The individual may not need training in all the units as some of these may have been covered in previous Leader Training and, will depend on the job being undertaken. The simple statement about deciding on appropriate training units means that 'if the individual can do it already, then training in that unit is not needed'.

Different training patterns

Scout Counties within the United Kingdom have developed different methods of provision for training requirements, but usually only one way is available in each County. All are equally valid and have been developed in response to the needs of participants in that area.

Some Counties will put on one continuous course to cover all of the areas outlined in the preceding tables. Alternatively, some will run each Training Unit as a stand alone course, whilst yet others will take some Units as core Units which all will attend while allowing choice for remaining topics. Sometimes a group of Units will be run as a weekend course. In addition to this there will be two further Units usually in the form of projects designed individually for each person.

Units 12 & 13 Projects

There will need to be discussion following completion of some or all of the earlier Units in order to decide what is required for completion of training. All members taking up new positions are required to undergo this job-specific training and personal assignments. It is likely that these projects will centre around the jobs that the individual will need to tackle and will be useful ways of putting training into practice whilst learning more. For the Group Scout Leader changing appointment this may turn out to be the only training required.

Note:
The publication referred to throughout this chapter – **Support for Training: Guidance and Information – Group Scout Leaders, Commissioners and Administrators**, is available from the Resource Centre at Gilwell Park.

INDEX

*References to the **Scout Group** and **Group Scout Leader** which occur throughout the book are not indexed.*

THE SCOUT ASSOCIATION COMMITTEE STRUCTURE

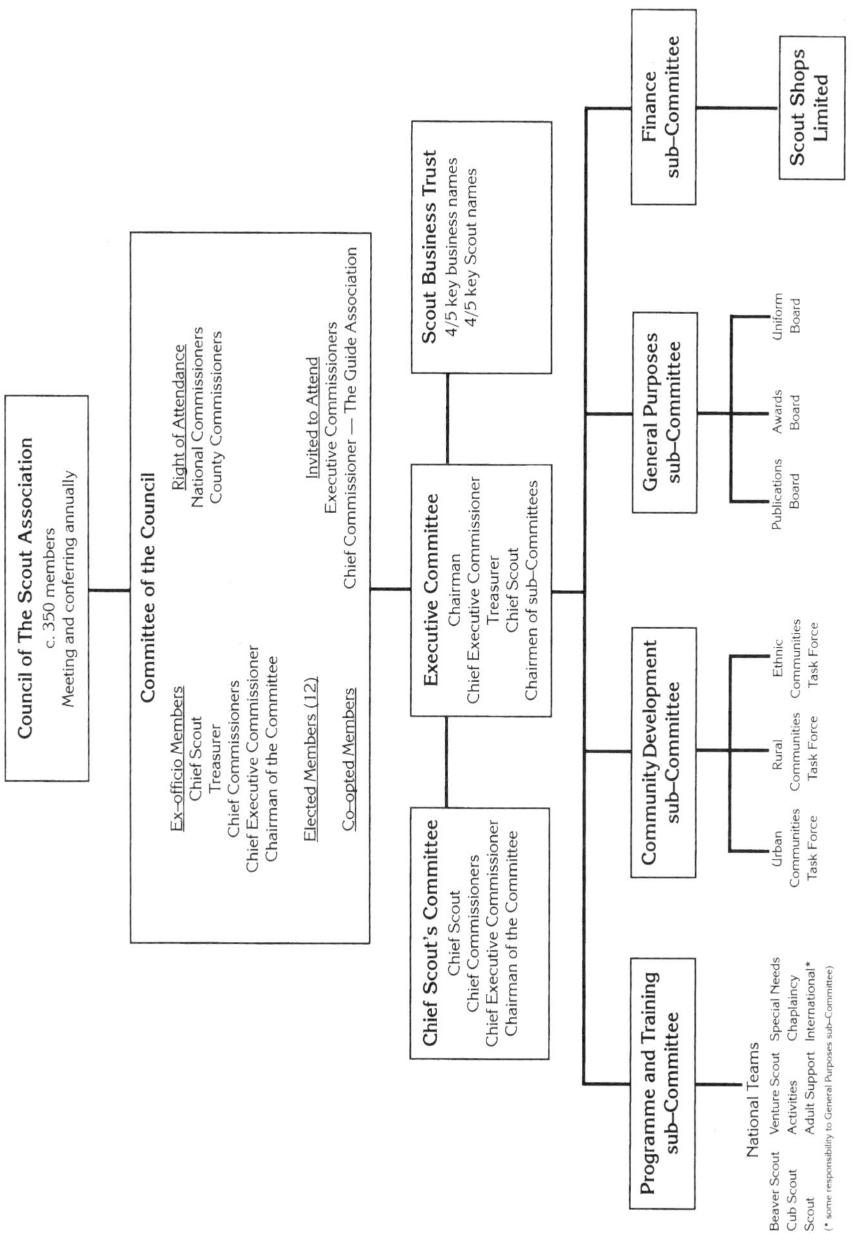

The Scout Association
Baden-Powell House
Queen's Gate
LONDON SW7 5JS
Tel: 0171-584 7030
Fax: 0171-590 5103

The Scout Association
Gilwell Park
Chingford
LONDON E4 7QW
Tel: 0181-524 5246
Fax: 0181-529 0994

The Scout Association
Churchill Industrial Estate
LANCING
West Sussex BN15 8UG
Tel: 01903-755 352
Fax: 01903-751044